REPRESENTATION AND RETRIEVAL OF VIDEO DATA IN MULTIMEDIA SYSTEMS

edited by

HongJiang Zhang
Hewlett Packard Laboratories

Philippe Aigrain
Universite Paul Sabatier

Dragutin Petkovic
IBM Almaden Research Center

A Special Issue of
MULTIMEDIA TOOLS AND APPLICATIONS
An International Journal
Volume 4, No. 1 (1997)

SPRINGER SCIENCE+BUSINESS MEDIA, LLC

MULTIMEDIA TOOLS AND APPLICATIONS

An International Journal

Volume 4, No. 1, January 1997

Special Issue on Representation and Retrieval of Video Data in Multimedia Systems
Guest Editors: HongJiang Zhang, Philippe Aigrain and Dragutin Petkovic

ISBN 978-1-4757-8273-8 ISBN 978-0-585-31786-1 (eBook)
DOI 10.1007/978-0-585-31786-1

Library of Congress Cataloging-in-Publication Data

A C.I.P. Catalogue record for this book is available
from the Library of Congress.

Originally published by Kluwer Academic Publishers in 1997
Softcover reprint of the hardcover 1st edition 1997

Printed on acid-free paper.

Multimedia Tools and Applications 4, 5 (1997)

Introduction to Special Issue on Representation and Retrieval of Visual Media in Multimedia Systems (2)

This is the second issue of the special issue of Multimedia Tools and Applications, devoted to Representation and Retrieval of Visual Media in Multimedia System, with the emphasis on implemented prototypes, tools and applications. This issue includes three papers focusing on video content analysis and representation. The first paper by Lee, Li, and Xiong presents an experimental video information management system. It describes briefly the video parsing subsystem for extracting low-level visual features of video data, and gives a detailed description on the conceptual clustering scheme implemented in the system for video content representation. The paper by Ardizzone and La Cascia reports a video indexing and retrieval system that supports automatic video structure parsing, shot feature extraction and content-based retrieval. Experimental results are discussed in detail. The last paper by Nack and Parkes presents a case study of the applications of a video semantics and theme representation scheme in automated editing and generation of humorous video from stock material. It addresses the problem of video editing modeling to realize a thematic specification by knowledge representation approaches, a very first step towards intelligent video editing.

While the works presented in these papers may be still preliminary, they have shown promising results in approaching many challenging research problems, which we believe will stimulate the work in this exciting new field. We hope you will enjoy reading this special issue.

Guest Editors:
HongJiang Zhang
Philippe Aigrain
Dragutin Petkovic

Multimedia Tools and Applications 4, 7–28 (1997)

VIMS: A Video Information Management System

JOHN CHUNG-MONG LEE, QING LI AND WEI XIONG
Dept. of Computer Science, Hong Kong University of Science and Technology, Clear Water Bay, Kowloon, Hong Kong

Abstract. Video data management is fast becoming one of the most important topics in multimedia databases. In this paper, we describe the development of an experimental video information management system, called "VIMS", being implemented at the Hong Kong University of Science & Technology, which employs two fundamental components—i) a Video Classification Component (VCC) for the generation of effective indices necessary for structuring the video data, and ii) a Conceptual Clustering Mechanism (CCM) having extended object-oriented features and techniques. By incorporating CCM concepts and techniques together with the classified features and indices generated from the VCC, the information management system enables users to form dynamically, among other things, video programs (or segments) from existing objects based on semantic features/index terms. A prototype of this system has been constructed, using a persistent object storage manager (viz., EOS), on Sun4 workstations.

Keywords: video database, video editing and classification, dynamic object clustering, extended object-oriented techniques, automatic video data structuring, camera break detection, and key frame selection

1. Introduction

With the onset of the information era and rapid progress in video technology, large amounts of video sources have become available. Video cassette tapes and laser-discs are used for many purposes such as entertainment, instruction, scientific recording, art storage, etc. However, this availability of video data is not synonymous with *accessibility* and *manipulability* of video data, the two most fundamental facilities needed from a video database. The reason for this is twofold. On the one hand, raw video data is not structured. For example, there are few or no temporal tags associated with video data, and traditional approaches do not provide powerful access to the video data from a video database. On the other hand, the conventional object-oriented database (OODB) modeling approach does not provide adequate support for video data management, which is, by nature, changing dynamically and incrementally. Thus, what are desired in an effective video database management system (VDMS) include:

i) structuring the video data and associating it with a rich set of indices to enable powerful access to the meaningful video segments of the video database, and,
ii) extending the conventional OODB approaches to facilitate dynamic creation, deletion and management of video data from the database.

1.1. An overview of related work

Many successful image databases have been developed. They can be divided into two categories, depending on the functionality of the system [1]. The first category consists of those databases that concentrate on retrieving an image according to one or more specific features. The second category of systems works mainly on retrieving requested information from a single image. In some systems, these two functionalities are combined. Most of these systems are based on the relational database approach.

More recently, a large amount of research activity has been focused on video databases. Compared with image databases, video databases are more challenging to work on because they are more complex and have more involved features. However, the entity relationship (ER) model for relational databases is not sufficient for describing video data, since it may involve complex objects as well as more relationships that can not be adequately accommodated by relational and ER modeling approaches. That is why object-oriented databases (OODBs) are being utilized as a better means due to their increased power of semantic modeling, in particular behavioral modeling and encapsulation, complex object support, type hierarchy and inheritance, and so on [23]. Despite these powerful features, conventional OODB systems are still not sufficient for video data management, particularly with respect to such subjective activities as video editing and production, which form the basis for facilitating the desired video data manipulability.

More specifically, video databases involve more issues to be resolved than text or image databases due to the following features:

1. Complex objects need to be defined and supported in a video DB since video data can take several different forms, e.g., frames, segments and programs. These objects are not independent; rather they share some inherent relationships in the form of "is-part-of" (or so-called composition) links.
2. From different points of view, the same image sequence may be given different descriptions. For example, given a specific video sequence, one user may be interested in its attributes, like color/BW or gun fighting/car racing. Another user may be more interested in whether it is a indoor or outdoor scene. However, it is impossible and inefficient to include all possible attributes in video DB when it is built.
3. The descriptions may be added or deleted dynamically. Suppose, for example, we have defined a sequence with several attributes like sound/no-sound, sports type, main roles, etc. But later on, we may no longer be concerned with certain attributes, say, sound/no-sound, and need other features for describing the sequence. Unfortunately, the conventional OODBMSs are not good at generating new classes dynamically.
4. Sharing of attributes (and values) or methods is often needed among video data objects, since meaningful scenes, in particular, may be overlapping or included in other meaningful scenes. For instance, we may describe Sequence A as being about U.S. President Bill Clinton's activities. We may also define Sequence B as being about Clinton's hobbies. Sequence B is actually a subset of A. Obviously, B will have some attributes that A has, say, they are both color and both outdoor scenes. On one hand, sharing among values and methods is very common. On the other hand, it is tedious to let users repeatedly

input the same information for different objects. However, conventional OODBMSs do not support the inheritance of attributes and their values or methods at object instance level.

In the following, we briefly examine some of the existing research in overcoming some of the shortcomings of conventional OODB systems, both in terms of video data modeling and video data management.

- Oomoto and Tanaka [18] proposed a schemeless object-oriented model. Their model allows users to (1) identify an arbitrary video frame sequence (a meaningful scene) as an independent object, (2) describe its contents in a dynamic and incremental way, (3) share descriptional data among video objects, and (4) edit author and abstract video objects. As their model is schemeless, the traditional class hierarchy of the object-oriented approach is not assumed as a database schema.
- Grosky et al. [5] proposed a content-based hypermedia (CBH) model. It is nothing more than an object-oriented schema over non-media objects that has undergone a transformation. They classified an object-oriented schema into three domains: class hierarchy, nested object hierarchy, and complex object hierarchy. Then they used meta-data classes to build various relations between objects, such as "is-part-of" and "appearing-in".
- Jain and Hampapur [8] proposed a video model (ViMod) based on studies of the applications of video and the nature of video retrieval requests. The features of their model include content dependence, temporal extent and labeling. A feature is said to be content independent if the feature is not directly available from the video data. Certain aspects of a video can be specified based on viewing a single frame in temporal intervals, whereas other features like motion can be specified only based on a time interval. The changes that occur in a video can be tracked over the extent of a time interval.

A follow-up challenge in developing any video information management system is the support of efficient and effective video management and access. In this context, we are aware of the following existing research work:

- Hirata and Kato [6] built a query system that uses visual examples, i.e., ART MUSEUM. A user has only to draw a rough sketch to retrieve the original image and all similar images in a database. The system evaluates the similarity between the rough sketch, i.e., visual example, and each part of the image data in the database automatically. This method is quite good from the viewpoint of users. However, there is a question about the system's effectiveness.
- Bimbo et al. [2] used Spatio-Temporal Logic to support the retrieval by content of video sequences through visual interaction. Temporal Logic is a language for the qualitative representation of ordering properties in the execution sequences of temporal systems. In their database, video sequences are stored along with a description of their contents in Spatio-Temporal Logic. Retrieval is supported through a 3D iconic interface.
- Little et al. [14] implemented a system that supports content-based retrieval of video footage. They define a specific data schema composed of movie, scene and actor relations

with a fixed set of attributes. The system requires manual feature extraction, and then fits these features into the data schema. Their data model and virtual video browser do not support queries related to the temporal ordering of scenes.

- Smoliar and Zhang [20] used a frame-based knowledge base method to support retrieval. They used frames to represent both classes (the categories) and instances (the elements categorized). In addition to the common techniques in frame-based knowledge base, they translated knowledge of a slot's type into knowledge of how to search it for retrieval purposes.

From the above observations, it is clear that meaningful video sequences are often identified and associated with their descriptional data incrementally and dynamically (after the video objects are stored in a video database). Therefore, it is important to accommodate video objects to have a flexible data structure that can be changed dynamically. In [13], we have proposed to advocate a dynamic object conceptual clustering video database model called CCM, which is based on Li and Smith's Conceptual Model for Dynamic Clustering in Object Databases [12]. Among others, this new model facilitates dynamic creation, deletion, and management of *ad hoc* object collections (called "clusters"), with a goal to complementing existing object-class power for accommodating generic application dynamics.

Related research works, on the video structuring aspect, have been at different levels. At the first level, some prototype systems proposed in the literature allow users to access desired images from image databases by directly making use of visual cues [9, 17, 19]. For example, in [17], Niblack et al. report that the QBIC system developed at IBM allows images to be retrieved by a variety of image content descriptors including color, texture, and shape. However, these prototype systems, even though they address the issues regarding the exploitation of spatial structure in images for effective indexing for retrieval, do not deal with video sequences where the temporal information also has to be considered. At the next level, video data structuring is viewed as segmenting the continuous frame stream into physically discontinuous units, generally called *shots*. In general, these physical units need to be clustered to form more semantically significant units, such as scenes. This so-called *story-based* video structuring has been used in video information browsing systems (eg., [13, 21]). The shots or scenes are described by one or several representative frames, known by the name *key frames* [11, 21, 29].

Camera breaks are usually characterized by brusque intensity pattern change between consecutive frames at the boundary. Several methods such as pairwise comparison, likelihood comparison and histogram comparison have been introduced [15, 27]. These methods have their merits and limitations. The histogram comparison method is insensitive to image movements since it considers intensity/color distribution—a statistical entity—between consecutive images. But it fails if the intensity/color distributions are similar because it ignores spatial information [10]. Both pairwise comparison and likelihood comparison make use of spatial information but the former is too sensitive to image movements and easily causes false alarms, whereas the latter suffers from computational complexity.

Based on the above observation, we have proposed a subsampling method called "Net Comparison" in [24]. It computes only a fraction of image pixels. It is accurate and fast because it uses both statistical and spatial information in an image and does not have to process the entire image. The size of the base windows (L) depends on the maximum non-(camera)break displacement (δ), which is the largest movement between two images. In [24], we conducted a statistical analysis showing that camera break detection with a low probability of error requires, in essence, checking only on a few, rather than on the complete set of base windows (small square regions). The number of the base windows required are also computed on the basis of the analysis.

We want to capture the *complete* content of video sequence using as few key frames as possible. How to find a systematic way to select key frames is a problem. There are few works relating to this subject in the literature. In [28, 29], a method (*robust*, according to the authors) was mentioned, but no details were given. In [22], for each shot, one key frame is selected at a predefined position in the shot. In [16], a representative video cut is selected as the first frame or the first subpart of each extracted cut. In [19], it has been suggested that key frames should be chosen according to color and motion (e.g., panning, zooming, object motion, etc.). No experimental results, however, were reported. In [26], the authors proposed a method to classify key frames of different shots using clustering techniques in order to establish semantic links between the shots.

In [25], we proposed a systematic method for selecting the key frame. The method includes a *Seek and Spread* algorithm and an image similarity measure using wavelets.

In the next subsection, we highlight the overall approach we have taken in the development of a flexible video database system called VIMS.

1.2. Our overall approach and system architecture

Figure 1 shows the system architecture of our VIMS prototype system currently being developed at the Hong Kong University of Science and Technology. It illustrates the

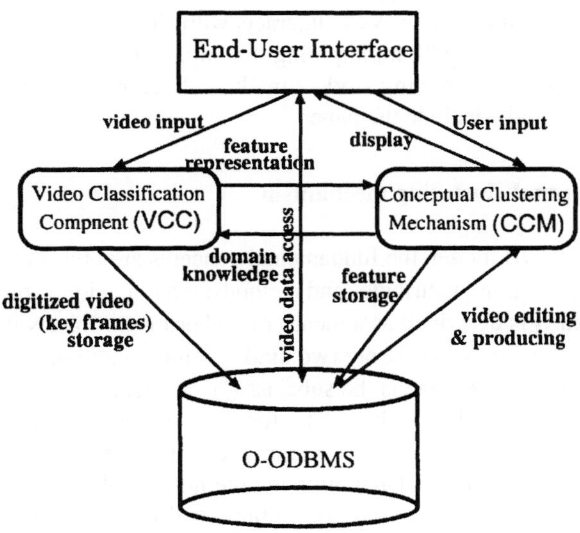

Figure 1. The architecture of VIMS Prototype System.

conceptual architecture of the prototype system, in which it is shown that there are two main development components on top of an object-oriented database. One is the Video Classifier Component (VCC), and the other is the Conceptual Clustering Mechanism (CCM). Both are connected to the underlying database and an upper front user-interface.

VCC partitions video into shots and select key frames for each shot (segment). From key frames, it extracts low level image features, such as color, texture, edge, shape, histogram, wavelet decomposition. We use wavelet coefficients of key frames to build a basic indexing system that supports direct access to the video data by the end-user. The usage of other features is decided by the message from CCM. Examples are shown in subsection 3.3.

CCM supports end-users to reorganize the video program dynamically using newly defined attributes. In this way, it is possible that different users can organize video data with different semantics or domain knowledge. This domain knowledge tells what and how features are used or grouped to form meta-level features in the VCC part. The relationship between VCC and CCM is bi-directional, since an edited video segment and/or package may lead to an enhanced classification or trigger a re-classification process, possibly using domain-knowledge supplied by users, to be activated. On the other hand, a newly classified result (feature representation) from VCC allows users to re-describe domain knowledge and trigger a classification process again.

1.3. Organization of the paper

The rest of the paper is organized as follows. In Section 2, we present the CCM portion of VIMS wherein we first discuss the problems with existing database models and then present the CCM model and its fundamental features to overcome those problems. In Section 3, we present the VCC portion of VIMS and the interaction between VCC and CCM. We first discuss the issues and goals of VCC in trying to structure the raw video data. Then an illustration of utilization of CCM applications is presented. Some examples are also given to provide a general picture of how VCC interacts with CCM. In Section 4, we present an experimental prototype of VIMS, highlighting the implementational issues, current status of VCC and CCM, and, the ongoing work. Finally, in Section 5, we summarize the scope of the VIMS project and conclude the paper.

2. CCM: Conceptual clustering mechanism

In a conventional OODB model, the fundamental concepts are object and class. An object represents an encapsulation of attributes and methods; it has a unique object identifier (Oid) in the OODB. A class is described as a means of gathering all objects that share the same set of attributes and methods. There are two kinds of inter-class relationships captured by a conventional OODB model; one is the subclass ("is-a") relationship and the other is the composition ("is-part-of") relationship. The former facilitates the notion of *inheritance* (i.e., a subclass may inherit the attributes and methods from its superclass as well as from its local additional ones), and the latter supports the notions of *existence dependency* and *component sharability* between a composite object and its component objects [13, 23]. Both types of inter-class relationships form class hierarchies that are useful for modeling video object relationships and data structure. For example, the composition hierarchy can accommodate the description of the structure of video data. In particular, a video program can be viewed as a composite object consisting of a sequence of frames that are component objects of the video program.

The main problems with the conventional OODB modeling approach are that a class has to be predefined statically, and objects of a class must be homogeneous in nature. Hence, such a model does not provide adequate support for those applications involving objects and inter-object relationships that are by nature *ad hoc*, irregular, tentative and evolving (as exemplified by video data objects). Extensions to the conventional OODB models are therefore needed in order to accommodate such advanced applications effectively.

In [12], a basic conceptual clustering mechanism (CCM) that facilitates dynamic creation, deletion, and management of *ad hoc* object collections (called "clusters") was defined, such that this mechanism can effectively accommodate more application dynamics, including various video data manipulations [13]. In this subsection, we describe the concepts as well as proper data structures of the CCM constructs that are suitable for flexible video data manipulation and management.

2.1. *The concepts of clusters and roles*

In CCM, a cluster consists of attributes, methods and a dynamic grouping of existing objects in the database, within which each object is assigned to one or more roles. More precisely, a cluster C_t is a dynamic object that has a tripartite form:

$$C_t = \langle A, M, X \rangle \tag{1}$$

where A is a set of cluster attributes, M is a set of cluster methods, and X is a set of the role-player associates:

$$X = \{\langle R_i : S_i \rangle \mid 1 \le i \le n\} \tag{2}$$

where R_i is a role, and S_i is a set of the objects that play that role within the cluster. Hence, the objects in S_i are called the "players" of the role R_i, and they are also the "constituents" of the cluster C_t. A role R_i can be described as follows:

$$R_i = \langle A_p, M_p \rangle \tag{3}$$

where A_p and M_p are a set of attributes and methods defined by the role R_i; these attributes and methods are applicable to the role players. A role R_i is active if the set of its methods (M_p) is not empty, otherwise it is a passive role. The players of a role may be "homogeneous"/"heterogeneous".

Clusters do not create or delete objects; they only include-in or exclude-out objects of databases. Therefore, they allow the user to form views over existing databases by tailoring at the cluster level without affecting the database itself. This is very useful and important for video data processing, such as video indexing and video production.

Clusters can establish a super-cluster/sub-cluster hierarchy similar to a composite hierarchy of classes. But a cluster may dynamically define its constituent objects and these objects can be of different types (heterogeneous).

Similar to classes that form an "is-a" hierarchy, roles can establish a super-role/sub-role hierarchy. A sub-role may inherit the attributes and methods (if any) of its direct and indirect super-roles. Furthermore, a sub-role can also define new properties and/or overwrite some of the inherited ones. Any objects playing the sub-role should be viewed as players of the super-roles. Examples of clusters and roles in video databases are given in Section 3.2.

2.2. *The data structures for clusters and roles*

To understand the concepts and feasible support of the cluster and role facilities better, we describe here suitable data structures that we have recently used, as a guideline for implementing such dynamic constructs.

Cluster tree. A cluster tree can internally be represented as a binary tree with a father pointer in each node. For example, the cluster tree in figure 2(a) is expressed as shown in figure 2(b). The father pointer is used to search all super-clusters of a specific sub-cluster quickly. The structure of each node in a cluster tree is illustrated in figure 2(c). Its type definition may be viewed as a meta-cluster. All application clusters of any user defined are instances of this meta-cluster. All cluster nodes in a cluster tree may be dynamically created, removed and modified by the user.

Since we cannot forecast how many attributes, methods and roles a user will define in a cluster, attribute-, method- and role-lists should be defined as dynamically linked lists. Their structures are illustrated in figure 3.

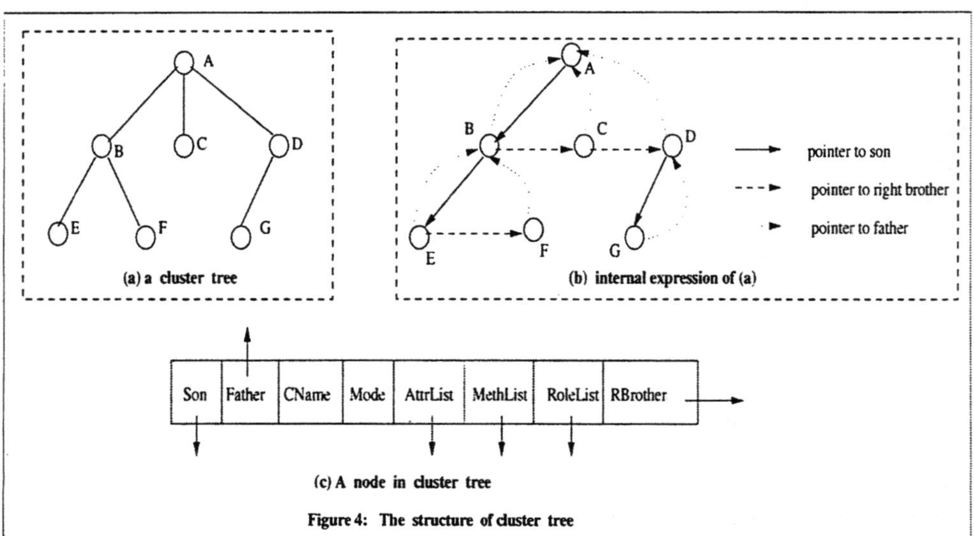

Figure 2. The structure of cluster tree.

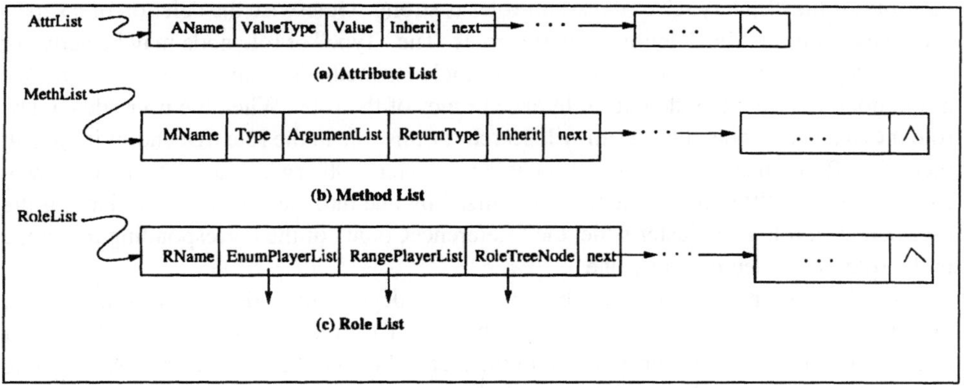

Figure 3. The linked-lists used in cluster node.

In the attribute list (figure 3(a)), "ValueType" is char, string, int, float, etc., and "Value" is a union type in order to save storage. "Inherit" indicates whether the attribute is inheritable by its sub-cluster or not. For a method-list (figure 3(b)), the "Type" is used to distinguish whether the method is a executable file or a library function. The "ArgumentList" is a linked list that stores the type of these arguments. The "ReturnType" is a type of return value if the method is a library function. "Inherit" determines whether or not a method may be inherited by its sub-clusters. Each role in the role list (figure 3(c)) has a set of players that are also the constituent objects of the cluster. These players may be added and removed dynamically. Hence they should also be dynamically linked lists. The players of a role may be of an enumeration and/or range form; thus we employed both "EnumPlayerList" and "RangePlayerList" to express these two types of players. The attributes and methods (if active) in a role are defined by some node of a role tree. Therefore, each role node in a role list has a "RoleTreeNode" pointing to a corresponding node of role tree.

In the enumeration type of the player-linked list, each node includes an object identifier (Oid) of the EOS. In the range type of player-linked list, each node includes the upper- and lower-limit of the players which are logically continuous.

Role tree. Similar to the cluster tree, a role tree is represented as a binary tree with a father pointer. The structure of each node in a role tree is shown in figure 4. Its type definition may also be viewed as a meta-role. All role nodes in a role tree are also created, deleted and modified dynamically by the user.

In figure 4, the attribute- and method-lists are the same as those of the cluster node mentioned above (viz., figures 3(a), (b)). The "LinkType" indicates the link manner (strong/weak) between a role and its super-role. The deletion of a super-role implies the deletion of its

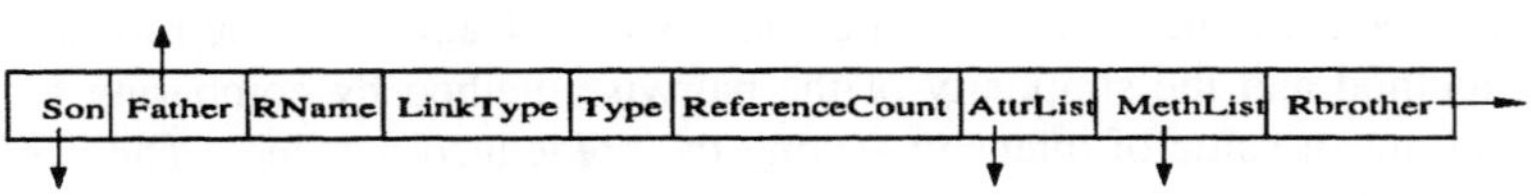

Figure 4. A node in role tree.

sub-roles if the "LinkType" of those sub-roles is strong. Otherwise the deletion of a super-role does not imply the deletion of its sub-roles. The "Type" of role node may be active or passive depending on whether or not the role includes methods. The "ReferenceCount" of a role node in a role tree denotes referenced times of the role. When the user adds a new role into a cluster node, the system will search for this role in the role tree and, if it finds it, then, the "ReferenceCount" is an automated increment. Otherwise the system adds a new role node whose "ReferenceCount" is initialized by one into the role tree. Similarly, if the user deletes a role in a cluster node, the "ReferenceCount" of the corresponding role node in the role tree is decreased by one.

The role node in a role tree may be created as independent or dependent of the role of the cluster. In other words, we may first establish the role tree and then establish the cluster tree; or first create the cluster tree and, in the meanwhile, create the role tree. A role node in the role tree is deleted if its ReferenceCount value is zero.

In next section, we disccuss how these CCM data structures help process video data in a specific context.

3. Incorporation of a video classification component in VIMS/CCM

As depicted in figure 1, another component of VIMS is the video classification component (VCC), which works closely with CCM. Basically, VCC has two functions: (1) structuring the video data; (2) extracting image features from key frames. Video data structuring is viewed as segmenting the continuous frame stream into physically discontinuous units, generally called *shots*, and clustering the shots into semantically significant units using key frames. We propose a subsampling method called *Net Comparison* for video segmentation and a method called *Seek and Spread* for key frame selection. We use wavelet decomposition and centered moment for the image similarity measure in key frame selection. Image features extraction, in our system, includes extracting color, texture, edge, shape and motion information from key frames using generic methods. The features are not extracted until the user specifies some features are needed for classifying some key frames. The user may also input some simple domain knowledge from CCM for the features extraction.

3.1. Video structuring in VCC

3.1.1. Video partitioning and key frame selection. The partitioning process consists of the detection of boundaries between uninterrupted segments (camera shots) that involve screen time, space or graphic configurations. These boundaries, also known as transitions, can be classified into two categories: gradual and instantaneous. The most common transition is camera breaks.

Besides the several existing methods for camera break detection, we also propose a method called Net Comparison (NC). It combines the advantage of the robustness of the histogram method and the simplicity of the pairwise method by comparing a statistical quantity—the mean value of intensity—along the predefined net lines. The *subsampling* approach compares pixels in predefined regions and inspects only a fraction of pixels. The *size* of the subsampling regions (L) depends on the maximum non-(camera)break displacement (δ), which is the largest movement between two images. The movement may be caused by an object moving, or by camera zooming, panning, etc. Obviously, we do not need to consider the movement of any small object in the image, such as bullets or rain drops, the speeds of which are usually very high. So velocity (δ) here means the movement of a sufficiently large region in the image between two consecutive frames. The *number* of subsampling regions we use in the method is computed by probability analysis [24]. We compare its performance with other existing algorithms and evaluate them on a large set of typical image sequences [24].

For the purpose of comparison, we have implemented four other methods for camera break detection: pairwise, likelihood, global histogram, and local histogram. Many experiments have been conducted on both color and black/white video. It turns out that the proposed method outperforms the others both in accuracy and in speed in our experiments [24]. This is because the method chooses an analyzed size of subsampling regions to make use of spatial information. Actually, pairwise, likelihood and local histogram methods all use spatial information; however, the areas they use are either too small (even one pixel) and therefore too sensitive or too large and so lose the spatial information. The reason why Net comparison is faster than the others is obviously due to its using only part of images instead of entire image.

3.1.2. Key frame selection and clustering. A continuous video is segmented into shots by partitioning. Each shot is represented by or abstracted into one or some frames, commonly called *key frames*. Key frames can serve two purposes: *browsing* and *computation of indices*. In retrieval by browsing, showing shots by simply using key frames as they are may confuse an untrained user rather than help him/her get the *story* or facilitate the retrieval. Like the table of contents of a book, shots must be organized into several levels of semantic abstraction. We call this *conceptual* or *semantic clustering*. The unit is *cluster*, which is a collection of semantically related shots and/or clusters [7, 13]. Now the question raised is how to find clusters, and to a lesser extent, how to choose key frames to represent them.

Basically, there are two issues related to key frame selection. One is the selection algorithm. Another is the image similarity measure or the definition of image distance.

For the selection approach, we propose a novel algorithm called *Seek and Spread*. The main idea is to search a key frame sequentially based on a similarity measure and extend (spread) the representative range of the key frame to the maximum. The image similarity measure is defined by wavelet coefficients that account for both spatial layout and detail content in an image. The coefficients from both scaling function and wavelet function are used (details are described in [25]).

3.1.3. Coupling of VCC with CCM. After partitioning video sequences and selecting key frames from each shot, VCC clusters the key frames and builds indices using predefined low level image features. Currently, we are using wavelet coefficients of each key frame to build the basic indexing. Ideally, there will be multiple levels of indexing (from low-level to semantic-level) and each level of indexing will be organized in terms of original "story semantics". Unfortunately this is not feasibly supported by present techniques. However, with our proposed architecture, it is possible to do so in an incremental fashion towards the direction; for example, (1) by keeping the order of the key frames and adding to each key frame a temporal tag; (2) by carefully pruning key frames for story continuity, etc. As mentioned earlier, CCM and VCC interact with each other. VCC provides CCM feature representation and basic indexing. CCM can dynamically introduce new user-defined attributes and more semantics for the video classification and VCC, therefore, can re-classify the video data more objectively and minutely and feed the new feature representation back to CCM. In subsection 3.2, we illustrate how CCM can be used to support video data processing effectively in a video database context. We will then present some examples in subsection 3.3.

3.2. Video data processing based on conceptual clustering

Firstly, we consider video indexing. As mentioned before, video classification enables video frames to be decomposed and grouped into segments. We will show that clusters are efficient means for describing video structure and indices derived from the video classification process of VCC. As an example, suppose Prog15 is a news program comprised of a sequence of news items, some commercial advertisements and a weather forecast. Through VCC's classification, Prog15 is decomposed into segments: Seg1, Seg2, Seg3, and Seg4, which represent local news, commercials, international news and the weather forecast respectively. Furthermore, Seg1 (local news) and Seg3 (international news) are broken into some sub-segments, say, Sseg11, Sseg12, ..., Sseg1k; Sseg31, ..., Sseg3i, ..., Sseg3j, each of which is a news item consisting of a sequence of frames. The structure of the news program Prog15 is constructed to a cluster tree as shown in figure 5(a), each node of which is a cluster. For nodes Seg3 and Sseg3i (which is a news item about a football game),

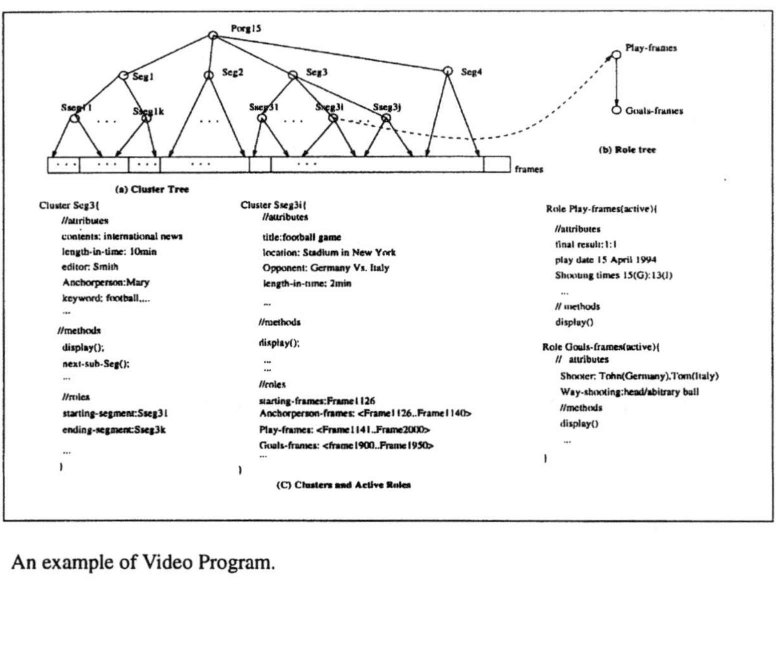

Figure 5. An example of Video Program.

their clusters' definitions are illustrated in figure 5(b). The cluster Sseg3*i* is the sub-cluster of Seg3. Obviously, most of the attributes and/or methods of Seg3 are not inherited by Sseg3*i*. If a sub-cluster inherits some properties from its super-cluster, we must explicitly specify which properties are inherited. For example, we may specify that the attribute "Anchorperson" in Seg3 is inherited by its sub-clusters.

We define four roles in cluster Sseg3*i*, two of which are active roles as shown in figure 5(c). These two active roles denote play- and goal-scoring scenes respectively. The role Goal-frames is a sub-role of the role Play-frames as shown in figure 5(b). In fact, super-roles and sub-roles also form a tree. Obviously, the attributes of the super-role Play-frames may be inherited by its sub-role Goal-frames. The method "display" is defined in cluster Sseg3*i*, role Play-frames and Goal-frames respectively. Although the names of the methods are same, the "display" of Sseg3 may display all frames in this cluster (i.e., Frame1126 ... Frame2000); whereas the "display" of role Play-frames only displays the frames of its player (i.e., Frame1141 ... Frame2000); similarly, "display" of role "goals-frames" only displays the frames of its player (Frame1200 ... Frame1240 and Frame1900 ... Frame1950). New attributes and methods may be added dynamically to these two roles for later use (e.g., we may add a method "slow motion" into role Goal-frames in order to watch goal-scoring scenes clearly).

Secondly, let us consider video (re-)production, where clustering techniques again prove to be very effective means for this type of activity. To us, video (re-)production is the creation of a new video program out of a collection of video segments that are pre-existing and/or newly produced.

Assume that we would like to produce a goal-scoring program out of various pre-existing news programs. We may search news programs from video databases and inspect each news program to see whether or not it contains video sequences of a football game. When a cluster representing a football game is retrieved, we extract the frames of scored goals out of this cluster to form a new cluster. A collection of such new clusters forms the program of "goal-scoring" as desired. For example, figure 6 shows a cluster (Seg5) extracted from cluster Sseg3*i* in figure 5(c). Users may add a variety of attributes and methods into the new cluster and their roles as desired in later processing phases (e.g., editing).

Although we only discussed video re-production that makes use of pre-existing video segments and frames, the same principle should also be applicable to producing video programs that involve newly shot segments. The difference here is that these new video segments need to be classified (into clusters and subclusters) by a classifier such as VCC before hand.

```
Cluster Seg5{
      //attributes
      opponent:      Germany Vs. Italy
      location:      Stadium in New York
      final result:    1:1
      play date:      15 April 1994
      shooter:      John(Germany),Tom(Italy)
        ...
}
```

Figure 6. An example of Video Production.

3.3. *Some examples*

Continuing the example of the last subsection, the user may define further clusters and roles in CCM; an example would be a role called Goal-frames. However, in the initial input from VCC (basic indexing), Goal-frames are not discernible from other frames. It is impossible to index all possible features in all frames. In VIMS, our goal is to provide as many generic features extraction methods as possible as part of VCC. These feature extraction modules are executed *only when required* by CCM. Also, the domain knowledge from CCM (provided by the user) can simplify and focus better on the feature detection. In our Goal-frames example, we may notice that one way to specify these frames is to identify all segments containing the penalty areas, or more simply, the goal post, because when shootings occur, the goal post is in general in the camera's view. A goal post is composed of two vertical bars and a horizontal bar. Due to viewpoint differences, the horizontal bar is seen as slanted most of the time. On the contrary, no matter what the viewpoint is, the two vertical bars are almost always vertical in the image plane. Thus we model the goal post as (two) vertical bar(s) in the image and then instruct VCC (through CCM) to extract all images containing two vertical bars. Moreover this detection can use generic edge detection and linking methods that are already implemented in VCC to suit the problem at hand. Here the images are indexed according to user specified semantics that are more application oriented than basic indexing. The idea has been applied to the video tape, "94 World Cup, 50 exciting shootings". Figure 7 shows some example images of Goal-frames detected.

In CCM, users usually only use high-level knowledge to define clusters and roles, but unless they like to extract interesting images manually, they have to instruct VCC how to extract the images in terms of low level features. A running example is to use color. People may define a role about some indoor scenes. The users may desire that in the scenes there is some special object, say a green sofa. Then they can tell VCC to extract images containing ranged sized green area. VCC can therefore apply color detection algorithm to do the job and thereby generate a semantic cluster of frames of indoor scenes containing a green sofa. Figure 8 shows some results of our experiments in searching for sofas in the images.

Figure 7. Localization of vertical bars for goal post detection.

Figure 8. Object searching with colors.

These two examples are just to illustrate the natural harmony and power of coupling CCM with VCC, as envisaged in the fundamental design of our VIMS system. It should be noted that the VIMS architecture can facilatate, through user interaction, multi-perspective, semantic-level clustering, and hence content-based retrieval in almost any situation. We are currently engaged in experimentation with other kinds of features like texture, motion, shape, etc.

4. An experimental prototype

As part of the research, we have developed an experimental prototype of VIMS. In this section, we give more details about the architecture of our VIMS prototype system. Also, we describe some implementation aspects of the CCM. At the end, we report current status of our experimental VIMS prototype.

4.1. Architecture and components of our prototype system

The current prototype of VIMS embodies a heterogeneous approach and environment in implementing the various components. As shown in figure 9, the VCC part is implemented in Visual C++ on a Pentium PC equipped with Targa_2000—a real-time frame grabber. The output of this component is then fed into the video database component, viz., the Video Base that is based on EOS—a persistent object storage manager developed at AT&T Bell Labs to support access to large objects by programs compiled with any C or C++ compiler such as the ones distributed by AT&T, SUN, GNU, and CenterLine [3]. The CCM is built on top of the Video Base and also the Method Base in which methods may be pre-existing video operation commands/functions provided by the VIMS, as well as those appended by the users. These methods can be invoked by roles/clusters, and any one method can be shared by several different roles/clusters. Note that the objects operated by methods of a role are the role's players who are corresponding clusters of component objects. Such objects, in general, are video materials in a video database. Therefore, the role can be viewed as the bridging mechanism between a video base and a method base.

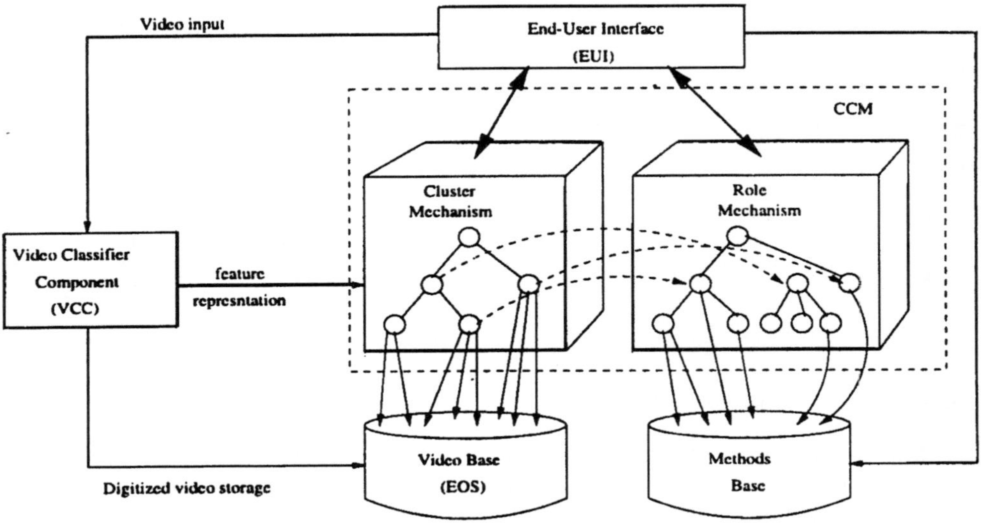

Figure 9. The components of VIMS prototype.

Also shown in figure 9 is a graphical user interface (GUI) through which the end-users interact with VIMS for video access and management. Among other features, the GUI provides the user with navigational facilities to browse the meta-data involved (i.e., the cluster- and role-trees). A structured query language is also being incorporated into it to facilitate both "declarative" and "feature-based" access to the video data [4]. Note that multiple clusters can be defined with respect to the same sequence of video data, so that *semantic relativism* can be also accommodated.

4.2. *Some further implementation issues on CCM*

In Section 2.2, we have already described suitable data structures for implementing the clusters and roles. In the remainder of this subsection, we will discuss some further implementation issues related to operating the cluster hierarchy, role hierarchy and dynamic execution of methods respectively. More details can also be found in [7].

4.2.1. The operations on the cluster- and role-tree. At present, cluster- and role-hierarchies are only tree structures, namely sub-clusters (sub-roles) and super-clusters (super-roles) are of a single-inheritance relationship. Generally, however, they are sufficient for video data processing because an existing object in a video database can play many different roles that are not in the same role hierarchy; similarly, an object can also participate in a variety of clusters that are not at all related.

Besides the dynamic creation, deletion and modification of a node in the cluster- and role-trees, the current prototype provides many basic operations as follows: it displays the structure of the cluster- and role-trees hierarchically; it displays all methods and attributes of a node in the two trees and inheritable ones of this node's ancestor nodes. A cluster node may display all its roles and those of the super-clusters. In these two trees, the user may find specified role- or cluster-nodes and identify their attributes, methods, member objects. These basic operations (methods) facilitate the creation, deletion and modification of the node in cluster- and role-tree, and addition, remove and modification of attributes, methods and member objects. For example, when the user adds attributes of role- and cluster-nodes, the system will invoke the method to display all the attributes of this node and inheritable attributes of its super-nodes. Thus the user knows which attributes have been defined or may be inherited to avoid repeating the definition. (Of course, the system can prompt the user if the definition is repeated.)

4.2.2. The execution of methods. As the prototype allows the user to include a set of methods into the cluster and roles dynamically, it greatly enhances dynamic characterization of clusters and roles. When including methods into a role or cluster, the user is required to provide the method name and the argument type, along with other details. While the user invokes a method from some role or cluster, the prototype will automatically display all methods (including inheritable methods of ancestor nodes) of this role or cluster to allow the user to choose the ones he/she desires.

The prototype supports two kinds of methods: one involves executable files, the other involves library functions. For the former, the prototype will invoke the method selected by the user through the UNIX system. For the latter, the process is more complex because the name of the function selected by the user is stored in a string as the value of this string, i.e., it is not an identifier denoted function-name and so the program can not invoke the function through this value. Fortunately, UNIX's C or C++ provides an interface of dynamic link programming. A Method Base (cf. figure 9) must be created for a shared object library by a compiler system. Thus our prototype can obtain the address of the function by a string of symbols and then invoke the function by its address. There exists a similar problem in passing arguments of function, however the C++ compiler only provides a means of obtaining the address of global variables by a string of symbols such that we can not find the address of a real-argument by string value if the real-argument is a local variable. This is sufficient in the context of VIMS because the executives of the methods are all video data such as frame, segment, etc., so that the prototype system may use Oids of EOS as arguments of invoking methods.

C++ allows the same name to denote different functions (i.e., overloading) such that the name of each function has a suffix in the internal symbol table generated by the C++ compiler. Hence our prototype must map the method names provided by the user into its internal expressions.

4.2.3. Storage and re-storage of cluster- and role-trees. In the current prototype, cluster- and role-trees are not stored in EOS in order to maintain the efficiency of system. The reason is that the structures of the two trees are rather complex, which imposes some difficulty for the EOS database kernel to operate efficiently.

In order to save memory, the prototype uses generalized lists as a storage structure of the trees. In particular, all information about the tree is converted into a character string by a set of recursive algorithms. The string is then stored in an external file. Restoring cluster-

and role-trees involves the creation of the trees and all the related linked lists, by reading and converting from strings from the corresponding external file.

4.3. *Current status*

At present, the basic functionality of the CCM component has been implemented and tested, and the VCC component has until now achieved the following functions:

1. Detects camera breaks in image sequences (i.e., scene changes).
2. Selects key frames in video shots.
3. Builds a table of contents based on key frames for the entire sequence of images.
4. Allows end-users to index any segment of the image sequence using key frames and/or key words.
5. Allows end-users to select an object/pattern in a frame manually and track or search for that object/pattern in image sequences based on color and/or edges.

Figure 10 shows some sample indices obtained using VCC from a video sequence together with the computer interface of the control panel for the laser disc player. We are currently engaged in developing further VCC algorithms to classify the various contents of video segments including scenes with moving objects, camera zooming and panning, complex road scenes, fade-outs, noisy scenes, videos with degraded quality and very dark

Figure 10. Screen layout of the VIMS prototype.

video images. These classified features will also be fed into VIMS to enhance its efficiency and the scope of its functioning.

5. Summary and concluding remarks

We have described in this paper the development of an experimental video database system called VIMS at HKUST. Our research activities concerning the two fundamental components—i) a Video Classification Component (VCC) for the generation of effective indices necessary for structuring the video data, and ii) a Conceptual Clustering Mechanism (CCM) having extended object-oriented features and techniques—have been presented.

The CCM portion of VIMS aims at overcoming the shortcomings of traditional relational database technology and conventional object-oriented database (OODB) approaches, especially in handling video data objects. The extension is centered around the notion of a conceptual clustering mechanism (CCM). Such extended clustering facilities allow *ad hoc*, irregular, tentative, and/or evolving video object collections ("clusters") to be dynamically formed, stored, and manipulated, thus various features of video data derived from video classification and/or managements can be represented and accommodated in a flexible manner. Further, clusters can impact on and interact with the constituents (i.e., video data objects) through the method defined by the active roles within the clusters. The utility of CCM in various managements of video objects has been discussed. We have also described some of the design and implementation issues of CCM as part of our VIMS prototype system (which has been developed on top of a persistent object storage manager).

The VCC portion of VIMS deals with effective structuring and indexing of the raw video data. Some techniques recently developed, as part of VCC, at our laboratory are presented. We briefly introduced our methods for camera break detection and key frame selection. The reationships between VCC and CCM are discussed. We have also shown how to take advantage of domain knowledge of underlying applications. Experimental results have been provided.

For the current prototype, there are several remaining issues that need to be addressed in subsequent research. For the VCC, we are going to do more experiments for testing and improving our methods. Some other features such as texture, shape, motion are to be used in our system. For the CCM, a plan is ongoing to extend the current cluster-/role-tree to be lattices, so that a cluster/role can be derived from multiple super-clusters/super-roles. We will also enrich the current method base to provide richer types of functions/operations for video data processing and management. One problem that must be addressed here is the support of passing arbitrary arguments, in order to provide flexible method definitions for the user. Also, a structured query language (extended Object-Oriented version of SQL) is being devised for CCM [4], which is to be ported and developed on top of VIMS. We plan to do these further developments in our VIMS prototype system, emphasizing *accessibility* and *manipulability*—two fundamental functionalities that the end-user would expect from a system like VIMS. Finally, we plan to test and refine our system by applying it in several real-life environments, including TV news room studios, university educational technology centers, and possibly public libraries.

Acknowledgment

The authors wish to express their sincere thanks to the anonymous referees who have made valuable suggestions that helped to clarify and improve the paper in several aspects. The authors are grateful to the Sino Software Research Center of the Hong Kong University of Science & Technology for supporting this research. Also, the authors thank Mr. Liu-Sheng Huang for the implementation of the CCM model, and Dr. Ruihua Ma and Dr. G. Sudhir for their contribution to this paper.

References

1. T. Arndt, "A survey of recent research in image database management," in Proc. IEEE Workshop on Visual Languages (Cat. No. 90TH0330-1), 1990, pp. 92–97.
2. A. Bimbo, E. Vicario, and D. Zingoni, "Sequence retrieval by contents through spatio temporal indexing," in Proc. IEEE Symposium on Visual Languages (Cat. No. 93TH0562-9), 1993, pp. 88–92.
3. EOS, Eos 2.1 User's Manual, Tech. Rep., AT&T Bell Lab., Murray Hill: New Jersey 07974, U.S.A., 1994.
4. C.W. Fung and Q. Li, "Versatile querying facilities for a dynamic object clustering model," in Proceedings of OOER'95: Object-Oriented and Entity-Relationship Modeling, 14th International Conference, Gold Coast, Australia, Dec. 13–15, 1995, pp. 77–88.
5. W. Grosky, F. Fotouli, I. Sethi, and B. Capatina, "Object-oriented databases: Definition and research directions," ACM SIGMOD Record, Vol. 23, 1994.
6. K. Hirata and T. Kato, "Query by visual example," in Advances in Database Technology EDBT'92 (Proc. of Third International Conference on Extending Database Technology), A. Pirotte, C. Delobel, and G. Gottlob (Eds.), Lecture Notes in Computer Science, Vienna, Austria, Springer-Verlag: Vol. 580, pp. 56–71, March 1992.
7. L.S. Huang, J.C.M. Lee, Q. Li, and W. Xiong, "An experimental video database management system based on advanced object-oriented techniques," in Proceedings of the SPIE—The International Society for Optical Engineering, Vol. 2670, pp. 158–169, 1996.
8. R. Jain and A. Hampapur, "Metadata in video databases," SIGMOD Record, Vol. 23, pp. 27–33, 1994.
9. T. Kato, "Database architecture for content-based image retrieval," in SPIE Proc. Image Storage and Retrieval Systems, Vol. 1662, pp. 112–123, 1992.
10. J.C.M. Lee and M.C. Ip, "A robust approach for camera break detection in color video sequence," in Proc. IAPR Workshop on Machine Vision Application (MVA'94), Kawasaki, Japan, Dec. 1994, pp. 502–505.
11. J.C.M. Lee, W. Xiong, D.G. Shen, and R.H. Ma, "Video segment indexing through classification and interactive view-based query," in Proceedings of Second Asian Conference on Computer Vision, Singapore, Dec. 1995, Vol. 2, pp. 524–528.
12. Q. Li and J. Smith, "A conceptual model for dynamic clustering in object databases," in Proc. 18th Intl. Conf. on VLDB, 1992, pp. 457–468.
13. Q. Li and J.C.M. Lee, "Dynamic object clustering for video database manipulations," in Proc. IFIP 2.6 Working Conference on Visual Database Systems, Lausanne, Switzerland, March 1995, pp. 125–137.
14. T.D.C. Little, E. Ahanger, R.J. Folz, J.F. Gibbon, F.W. Reeve, D.H. Schelleng, and D. Venkatesh, "A digital on-demand video service supporting content-based queries," in Proc. First ACM Intl. Conf. on Multimedia, 1993, pp. 427–436.
15. A. Nagasaka and Y. Tanaka, "Automatic video indexing and full-video search for object appearances," in IFIP Proc. Visual Database Systems, II, E. Knuth and L. Wegner (Eds.), IFIP, Elsevier Science Publishers B.V.: (North-Holland), 1992, pp. 113–127.
16. A. Nagasaka, T. Miyatake, and H. Ueda, "Video retrieval method using a sequence of representative images in a scene," in Proceedings of IAPR Workshop on Machine Vision Applications, Kawasaki, Japan, Dec. 1994, pp. 79–82.

17. W. Niblack, R. Barber, W. Equitz, M. Flickner, E. Glasman, D. Petkovic, P. Yanker, C. Faloutsos, and G. Taubin, "The QBIC project: Query images by content using color, texture and shape," in SPIE Proc. Storage and retrieval for image and video databases, 1993, Vol. 1908, pp. 173–186.
18. E. Oomoto and K. Tanaka, "Ovid: Design and implementation of a video-object database system," IEEE Trans. on Knowledge and Data Engineering, Vol. 5, pp. 629–643, 1994.
19. A. Pentland, R.W. Picard, and S. Scaroff, "Photobook: Tools for content-based manipulation of image databases," in SPIE Proc. Storage and retrieval for image and video databases II, 1994, Vol. 2185, pp. 34–46. "Longer version available as MIT Media Lab Perceptual Computing," Technical Report No. 255, Nov. 1993.
20. S.W. Smoliar and H.J. Zhang, "Content-based video indexing and retrieval," IEEE Multimedia, Vol. 1, pp. 356–365, 1994.
21. Y. Tonomura, "Video handling based one structured information for hypermedia systems," in Proc. ACM Int'l Conf. on Multimedia Information Systems, New York, USA, ACM Press, 1991, pp. 333–344.
22. H. Ueda, T. Miyataka, and S. Yoshizawa, "IMPACT: An interactive natural-motion-picture dedicated multimedia authoring system," Proc. Human Factors in Compating Systems CHI'91, 1991, pp. 343–350.
23. K.W., E. Bertino, and J.F. Garza, "Composite object revisited," in Proc. of ACM SIGMOD Intl. Conf. on Management of Data, 1989, pp. 337–347.
24. W. Xiong, J.C.M. Lee, and M.C. Ip, "Net comparison: A fast and effective method for classifying image sequences," in Proceedings of the SPIE—The International Society for Optical Engineering, San Jose, CA, USA, Feb. 1995, Vol. 2420, pp. 318–28. Storage and Retrieval for Image and Video Database III.
25. W. Xiong, J.C.M. Lee, and R.H. Ma, "Automatic video data structuring through shot partitioning and key frame selection," Machine Vision and Application: Special issue on Storage and Retrieval for Still Image and Video Databases (1996), (submitted), (Technical Report HKUST-('S96-13).
26. M. Yeung, B.L. Yeo, W. Wolf, and B. Liu, "Video browsing using clustering and scene transitions on compressed sequences," in Conf. on Multimedia Computing and Networking, Vol. 2417, 1995, Proceedings of the SPIE—The International Society for Optical Engineering, 1995, pp. 399–413.
27. H.J. Zhang, A. Kankanhalli, and S.W. Smoliar, "Automatic partitioning of full-motion video," ACM Multimedia Systems, Vol. 1, pp. 10–28, 1993.
28. H.J. Zhang, C.Y. Low, Y.H. Gong, and S.W. Smoliar, "Video parsing using compressed data," in Proceedings of the SPIE—The International Society for Optical Engineering, San Jose, CA, USA, Feb. 7–9, 1994, Vol. 2182, pp. 142–149. Image and Video Processing II.
29. H.J. Zhang and S.W. Smoliar, "Developing power tools for video indexing and retrieval," in SPIE Proc. Storage and retrieval for image and video databases II, 1994, Vol. 2185, pp. 140–149.

John Chung-Mong Lee received his Ph.D. in Computer Science from the University of Minnesota in 1989. From 1989 to 1992 he worked as a research member of the Institute of Systems Science at the National University of Singapore. He joined the HKUST Department of Computer Science in June 1992. He received Digital's Alpha Innovators Award in 1993. Dr. Lee has a patent and a pending patent in vehicle and container number recognition systems. At present, he leads a group of researchers working on an intelligent video manipulation project called VIMS. His reseach interests include computer vision, image processing, pattern recognition, and multimedia.

Qing Li received his B.Eng. from Hunan University, China in July, 1982, and M.Sc. and Ph.D. degrees (both in Computer Science) from the University of Southern California in May 1985 and December 1988, respectively. He was a Lecturer at the Department of Computer Science, Australian National University from 1989 to 1991. He joined in 1992 the newly founded Hong Kong University of Science and Technology as an assistant professor in the Department of Computer Science. His research interests include semantic modeling, object migration and schema evolution, database integration and federation, and video/multimedia databases.

Dr. Li is a member of the Association of Computing Machinery and the IEEE Computer Society. He has served as a program committee member for VLDB, OOER, DASFAA, IFIP Database Semantics conferences, among several other interanational and regional conference/workshops.

Wei Xiong received his B.S. in 1984 and M.S. in 1987 in computer science from Tianjin University, China. He is currently a Ph.D. candidate in the Department of Computer Science at Hong Kong University of Science and Technology. From 1987 to 1993, he served as a lecturer in the Department of Computer Science and Engineering at Tianjin University. His research interests include video database, computer vision, image processing and pattern recognition.

Multimedia Tools and Applications 4, 29–56 (1997)

Automatic Video Database Indexing and Retrieval

EDOARDO ARDIZZONE ardizzone@Odiepa.unipa.it
MARCO LA CASCIA lacascia@Odiepa.unipa.it
Department of Electrical Engineering, University of Palermo, Palermo, Italy

Abstract. The increasing development of advanced multimedia applications requires new technologies for organizing and retrieving by content databases of still digital images or digital video sequences. To this aim image and image sequence contents must be described and adequately coded. In this paper we describe a system allowing content-based annotation and querying in video databases. No user action is required during the database population step. The system automatically splits a video into a sequence of shots, extracts a few representative frames (said r-frames) from each shot and computes r-frame descriptors based on color, texture and motion. Queries based on one or more features are possible. Very interesting results obtained during the severe tests the system was subjected to are reported and discussed.

Keywords: content based retrieval, video databases, features extraction

1. Introduction

Digital images and video are becoming a component of computer and telecommunication usage of ever-increasing importance. Content-based technology for indexing and retrieval is then required to effectively use these digital repositories. Application areas in which content-based retrieval is becoming a principal activity are, among others, TV productions, video on demand, home entertainment, art galleries and museum management, architectural and engineering design, geographic information systems, and so on [16].

Other applications are related to the development of information superhighways. When the bandwidth needed for interactive multimedia will be available at home, each user could access a remote server containing very large image and video databases. In this scenario content-based retrieval assumes a fundamental role. Also Multimedia Information Systems [15] can benefit of content-based retrieval technology; although they will mainly provide techniques to manage and distribute large amounts of multisource multimedia information, automatic indexing of images and video still plays a central role.

Previous approaches to image indexing and content-based retrieval are mainly based on features manually described by an operator. Images and videos are then treated as large binary data sets related to these manually described attributes. Retrieval is performed within the framework of conventional DBMS. Only in recent years research has focused on the use of internal attributes of images and videos computed in an automatic or semi-automatic way [14, 22, 35, 58]. Anyway images and videos are usually characterized during the DB population. Two different archives are managed, the one containing raw-data, the other containing features.

During a database population session a new video or image is added to the DB, its content is adequately coded based on the data model used. This step should be as automatic as possible due to the large amount of data to be inserted. However it should be noted that some manual annotation is still essential if the application requires retrieval be related also to traditional features, e.g., object names, dates, and so on.

During a database querying session the user performs a query to retrieve the desired video from the DB. Typically the user works in an iterative way. Queries may be direct or by example.

Depending on the used data model direct queries may be based [16] on sketch, objects-shape, texture, color, text, and so on.

In the following we refer to images to indicate either single images, in the case of still image databases, or representative frames, i.e., frames representing a sub-part of a video sequence in the case of video databases.

To specify a query by sketch the user makes a freehand drawing of the dominant lines and edges in the desired image. In the case of a query by shape the query specification is a drawn shape. Area, circularity, eccentricity, major-axis direction and others are the features typically used to match shapes. Queries by texture are based on texture features that are mathematical representations of contrast, coarseness and directionality. An user can put such a query by selecting the numerical range for these features. Color queries are mainly based on color histogram matching; to specify a query the user may select a few color percentages or search for a dominant color. Queries by text are typically based on keywords associated with the image or video during the population step.

A better interaction is allowed by querying by example; the user should only insert an image and the system returns the n best matching images from the archive, with n chosen from the user.

Other systems [7, 46] use different techniques in the characterization step; they don't compute an a priori set of features to allow more specific queries. However a such approach is computationally expensive and tends to be used only for small specific image databases and when retrieval is performed exclusively by domain experts.

In each case the automatic extraction of features is a fundamental task. Manual entry of content descriptions is tedious, time-consuming, expensive and subjective, thus users enter only the minimum annotations necessary to accomplish a specific task. This makes unpractical or useless the large databases containing several thousands of images. For these reasons, in the last years more convenient approaches have been attempted, based on the automatic extraction of salient features from images and videos, borrowing methodologies and tools from classic areas of computer vision and from image analysis.

This paper detailly describes the indexing and querying capabilities of JACOB, a content-based storage and retrieval system for video databases [23]. The key properties of JACOB are related to its capability of automatic indexing of domain independent videos, so that the system could result particularly suited for storage and retrieval of TV sequences.

In Section 2, we address recent related work. In Section 3, we describe the general architecture of our system. The database population step and the features used to characterize the videos are described in Section 4. In Section 5, we show the query processing techniques we developed and discuss experimental results obtained for several sample queries put to a database of significant size. Section 6 includes concluding remarks and future direction.

2. Related work

In the last years several content-based image and video retrieval systems have been developed. These systems differ in terms of features extracted, degree of automation reached for feature extraction and level of domain independence.

The QBIC system [13, 14, 24, 25] is a system treating both images and video. The data model has scenes (full images) that contain objects (subsets of an image), and video shots that consist of sets of contiguous frames and contain moving objects. Representative frames (r-frames) are generated for each shot. R-frames are treated as still images but further processing of shots generates motion objects. Scenes and objects are described in terms of color, texture, shape and motion. Both direct queries and queries by example are allowed.

An integrated solution for video parsing and content-based video retrieval and browsing has been presented in [58]. Video parsing consists in temporal segmentation of a video into single camera shots, abstraction of each shot into key-frames, and content extraction from key-frames, driven by visual features like color and texture. Temporal shot characteristics, such as camera operations and temporal variations of brightness and colors, are also extracted. Retrieval and browsing are based on key-frame features, temporal shot features, or a combination of the two. The system can also operate on compressed (MPEG) video.

The OVID [34] system uses an original data model called Video Object Data Model. A video object is an arbitrary frame sequence (a meaningful scene). Each video object has attributes and attribute values describing its content. Moreover the video object data model is schemaless and inheritance based on interval inclusion relationship is introduced to share descriptional data among video objects. The video characterization takes place at high level and is done manually.

VisualSEEk [43] is a content-based query system allowing for querying by color and spatial layout of color regions. *VisualSEEk* represents the global color information using color histograms and provides histogram similarity measures for comparing the image color features. Tools for annotating images and for searching archives using text are also provided.

CHABOT [33] allows for the storage and retrieval of a vast collection of digitized images. One of the goals in the CHABOT system is to integrate image analysis techniques into text-based retrieval systems.

The CANDID system [21, 22] is a content-based storage and retrieval system of digital images. For each image a global signature comprising texture, color and shape information is automatically computed. Queries are specified by example.

The VISION system [26] is devoted to efficient creation and exploration of digital video libraries. A two-step algorithm, based on first the video and then the audio contents, is used to segment videos into a number of logically meaningful clips. Video-based segmentation is achieved using the absolute difference of the color histogram between successive frames. Audio-based post processing allows for the correction of falsely detected shot boundaries, even in presence of editing effects.

Also the CMU approach to digital video libraries [9] is based on the collaborative interaction of image content and speech and natural language understanding.

Browsing and retrieval in large digital video libraries are the main goal of some approaches based on non-linear descriptions of video content. In [53–55] clustering of similar shots is proposed. Compressed video sequences are initially analyzed to identify both abrupt and gradual shot transitions. Similarity measures of images, based on color and luminance information, are then used to build shot clusters with an adjustable tolerance degree. A shot cluster is considered a scene. A hierarchical scene transition graph, i.e., a collection of directed graphs, is then used to model the video structure, with no *a priori* knowledge of the story. Each node of the graph at the lowest level of the hierarchy represents a scene, and edges represent the progress of the story from a scene to the next. Thus browsing is based on both visual content (and temporal variations) of shots and video structure.

A structured conceptual schema for movie data based on a graph-like model is proposed also in [11, 12]. This hypermedia system exploits both a feature extraction engine, able to automatically detect some of the production characteristics of a movie, such as editing operations, and a user-guided iconic interface, that enables complex queries to be formulated, even without the knowledge of any formal query language.

Other systems [7, 35, 45, 56] are more task-oriented; several of them have been proposed for storage and retrieval of faces. However these systems are usually extensible to other classes of images. In [42], a method for shape-based searching in image databases is described that uses deformable prototypes to represent categories. The technique of modal matching is employed to compare shapes in terms of nonrigid deformations with respect to a small subset of representative prototypes.

JACOB, the indexing and retrieval system that is described in the rest of this paper, belongs to the class of general purpose systems and is able to treat both still images and video. Features automatically extracted are based on color, texture and motion. A preliminary version of JACOB was described in [23].

3. The general architecture of the proposed system

The JACOB system has been developed at the Computer Science and Artificial Intelligence Lab of our Department. A WWW demo is also available at the URL: http://wwwcsai.diepa.unipa.it. The JACOB system has been developed in a highly modular way to facilitate future work and improvement. Like other related systems, JACOB has an architecture that can be subdivided into two functional units: the first one is dedicated to the database population and the second one to the database querying. The user interaction is necessary only during the querying phase; the population phase, in the current implementation, is completely automatic.

The system operation is summarized in figure 1. The videos are split in short sequences called shots by the shot extractor. A few representative frames (said r-frames) are therefore selected from each shot and described in terms of color and texture content. These are *static* descriptors. Motion features related to short, 9-frame sequences in which r-frames are embedded are also computed to give a *dynamic* description of the r-frame. The r-frame selection and the computation of color, texture and motion features are performed by the feature extractor module. Shots and r-frames are stored in the raw-data DB. Features are stored in the feature DB.

When a query, direct or by example, is put to the system, the query processor module interprets it and arranges the query parameters for the operation of the match engine module.

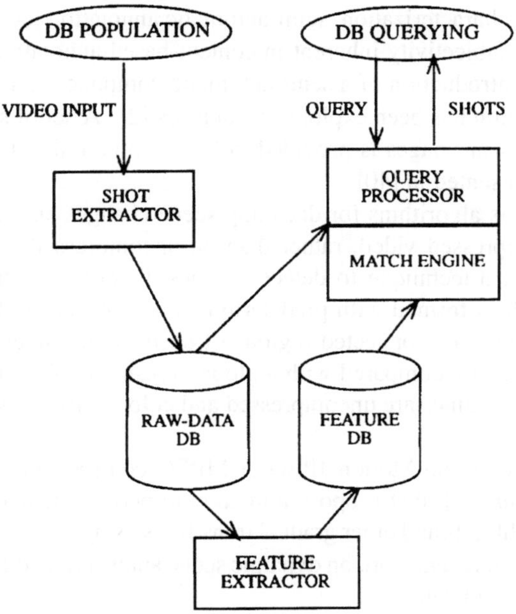

Figure 1. General architecture of the JACOB system.

The match engine searches for the best similar shots by analyzing the data stored in the feature DB. The n most similar shots, with n chosen by the user, are rendered. The user can browse the resulting shots and can iterate the query, changing if necessary the query parameters (only on the selected shots). This technique leads to a simple and fast retrieval of the desired shot.

4. DB population

In the current implementation, this step is automatically performed to allow the insertion of large videos at low cost. The input to the system is a digital video in industrial standard format (MPEG or QuickTime). Once uncompressed, the video is processed by the shot extractor.

The choice of a fully automatic operation is not the only possible. Manual annotation is necessary, alone or complementary to automatic one, when retrieval has to be grounded on traditional, non visual features (object names, specific object instances, places, dates, etc.), of the kind directly related to keywords or labels in traditional DB operations. Current technology is not able to automatically extract such *semantic* features from raw image data, with the exception of few, strictly domain depending applications (see for example [3], where low-level visual features are treated as knowledge elements in the context of an autonomous robotic system, with the heavy implication of artificial intelligence and knowledge representation techniques).

When the interaction with the user may allow the system to *learn* about the user interpretation of significant aspects of the input sequence, e.g., related to image segmentation, object detection and motion characterization, semi-automatic annotation tools may be introduced in order to face with subjectivity inherent in content-based annotation and retrieval tasks (see also [36]). The introduction of a semi-automatic component for shot labelling based on global camera motion has been explored by authors [2]. A set of semi-automatic tools for identifying objects in images is provided in [14], while assisted image segmentation based on texture is presented in [40].

Rapid scene analysis algorithms for detecting scene changes and other interesting features directly on compressed video, rather than on uncompressed sequences, have been also proposed. In [6], a technique to detect changes directly on intra-frame JPEG data is presented. A vector is formed with predetermined ac coefficients from the 8×8 DCT blocks in a fixed number of connected regions of each frame. Inner products of vectors from successive frames are compared with a global threshold. When closed to the threshold, a few neighboring frames are uncompressed and color histograms are used for further analysis.

Scene change detection on Motion JPEG or MPEG compressed streams has been explored by Yeo and Liu [52], that propose a method to perform temporal segmentation of videos and detect flashlights and other gradual transitions using the dc sequences. They also present a good review of recent work on dynamic scene analysis and other image processing operations on compressed data.

4.1. Shot detection

As above mentioned, the first step of video processing for database population consists in segmenting the input video into shots. To this aim a scene cut detection method is required.

Besides the above mentioned work of Yeo and Liu, several methods have been proposed in the literature, for detection of both abrupt changes and gradual transitions, due to editing effects. Zhang et al. [57] propose a threshold method working on differences of color histograms. They also deal with special effects, such as dissolving sequences, making use of a double threshold technique. A smaller threshold is used to first detect the start of the special effect. The corresponding frame is marked and compared to successive frames to test if a second threshold is exceed (corresponding to a change). If on the contrary the intermediate frame-to-frame difference drops below the first threshold, no change is declared.

In [29] various comparison techniques, e.g., differences of gray-level or various difference metrics of color histograms, are tested, with some correction factor introduced against short-time noise like camera flashes. Other special effects are not taken into account.

Hampapur et al. [17, 18] present a model-based method, inspired to well established video production processes, able to capture various kinds of shot transitions. In particular, video segmentation is formulated as a production model-based classification problem, and segmentation error measures are also defined.

Aigrain et al. [1] also use a rule system for video segmentation. Rules deal with temporally located information present in video frames. If adequately combined, these rules allow for identification of more macroscopical changes in the frame sequence and subsequent segmentation.

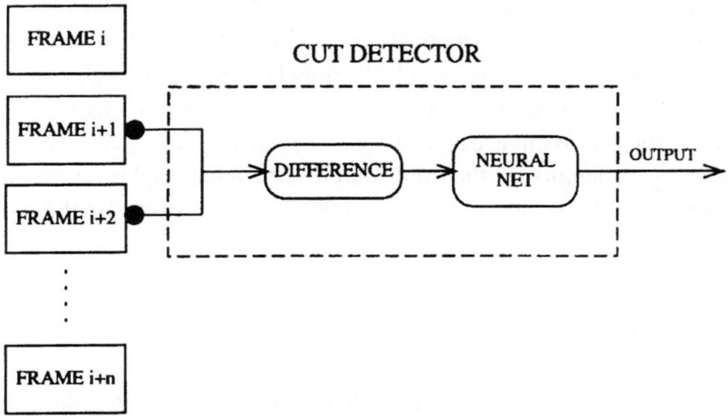

Figure 2. The shot detector.

Another model-based technique has been presented in [10, 11]. Here, video segmentation focuses on editing procedures during movie production, where editing phase contributes in a crucial manner to the creation of a semantics. The used model is a mathematical abstraction of this "paradigm of editing".

In the present work we use the technique, employing also a neural network, detailly described in [4]. Essentially, to detect a scene cut two successive frames are preprocessed and a pixel-by-pixel difference is computed. This difference is then processed by a multi-layer perceptron that determines if the two frames belong to the same shot.

More particularly (see also figure 2), the proposed approach consists of two main steps: the first one is a fast on-line frame preprocessing, the second one is represented by the neural network operation. In the current implementation, color information present in input sequences is discarded and only luminance is used for the cut detection.

Since dimensions of input images can vary, in the preprocessing stage each $M * N$ image is resized to obtain a $16 * 16$ gray-level (8-bits) image; these dimensions define the inputs to the net.

The pixel-by-pixel difference of the reduced images corresponding to two successive frames is therefore sent as input to the net. Gray levels are normalized to fit the 0–1 range.

Despite of its simplicity, this approach leads to satisfactory results, and exhibits a good behavior with respect to the speed requirements posed by the neural network. The used neural architecture is able to process several hundreds of frames per second, thus far exceeding the requirements of the whole system.

The proposed architecture implements a two-layer perceptron net with a learning algorithm based on the conjugate gradient descent method (CGD), following the recursive formulation first developed by Powell [41].

In order to make the generalization capability of the net adequate to domain-independent scene cut, it is necessary to have a large data set for the net off-line training. To this aim, and for testing purposes, a few thousand frames taken from videos directly acquired from TV broadcast, the QuickTime movie (infobahn) available on Macintosh System 7.5 CD and some freeware videos, available by anonymous ftp around the WWW were used.

Experimental results show that the method is fast and reliable. The net handled correctly all the cut occurrences within the videos we used. Just two false cuts were detected. Cuts are correctly detected even in presence of little global changes from a shot to the successive one, and high motion cases are correctly classified as no-cut situations.

Editing effects (fades, dissolve, ecc...) are not currently addressed by the system, while a change of intensity or position of the light sources, or a local brightness variation between two frames due to a relative scene-camera motion are recognized by the net as a no-cut situation.

4.2. R-frame selection

Choice of r-frames[1] is a crucial task in automatic video annotation, since their visual features are essential for shot indexing and retrieval. R-frames must capture the low level semantics of the shot, in this sense they must allow for a description as precise and complete as possible. On the other hand, it should be profitable to maintain low the size of data needed for computation. In other words, a good representation of a shot in terms of r-frames must strike a balance between adequateness and concision of description.

Several attempts have been accomplished to get this goal, also based on more or less simple heuristics. Early work [6, 29] generally assumed a single key-frame per shot, for example the first frame in the sequence. This choice can be misleading, because two shots of similar content may be considered to be different if representative frames are different. In other cases, the first and the last shot frame have been proposed as representative frames.

Generally speaking, assuming a fixed number of representative frames per shot is not a good idea, because this can give problems of oversampling for shots with slow dynamics, while one or two r-frames may be not sufficient to accurately describe a shot where camera or object motion is noticeable.

In a preliminary version of this work, we tried to overcome this problem adopting this simple solution: if the video shot is shorter than one second then only a frame is chosen as r-frame (the middle one). If the shot is longer than one second then a r-frame for each second is chosen. However such a technique, like the ones above mentioned, has a heavy drawback: the shot content is not at all taken into account, only its length is assumed as significant.

On the contrary, both motion and visual features are important for shot description. Motion has been used to identify r-frames in [51], where optical flow analysis allows to measure the motion in a shot and select r-frames as the local minima of motion. In principle, this technique should permit to select the number of representative frames appropriate to the shot composition.

In [58], the r-frame extraction process is integrated with the process of segmentation, and utilizes only information computed by the last one. In particular, both color features (color histogram, average brightness, mean and moments of color, dominant color) and motion features (dominant motion components) are used, also directly on compressed data.

Yeung and Liu [53] propose each shot be described by a representative image set, i.e., a good but nevertheless greatly subsampled frame collection. The selection of the representative set is achieved by non-linear temporal sampling, which measures the dissimilarity (by color histograms and luminance projections) between the last selected frame and the remaining frames, selecting only frames with considerable variations.

We adopted a simplified technique of non-linear temporal sampling, based on the comparison of a cumulative difference of frame brightness values with a threshold. In particular, the algorithm scans the input sequence, that is made up by n frames, and operates in the following way:

1. Initialize to 0 the variable *fc* (frame counter) and set the variable T to the threshold value.
2. Initialize to 0 the variable *sum* (the difference accumulator).
3. Assume the current frame is a r-frame.
4. While $sum < T$ do
   (a) Increment *fc*.
   (b) If $fc = n - 1$, then go to 5, else calculate the pixel-by-pixel difference between the brightness of the current frame and the previous one, compute the average and sum this value to *sum*.
5. End.

In the current implementation the threshold value has been tuned experimentally.

The technique has been tested during the population of the DB used for the experimentation on JACOB, giving surprisingly good results, despite of some inherent defects due to its simpleness, such as the color information not at all taken into account. About 500 shots were considered, giving about 1500 r-frames, with a resulting frequency of about 3 r-frames per shot. This value indicates perhaps a tendency to a small oversampling. However, even if no explicit motion analysis is carried out, the algorithm is effective in selecting a low number (1 or 2) of r-frames for still shots, while up to 6 r-frames were selected for shots with noticeable motion.

To further evaluate the behavior of our r-frame selector, a performance analysis based on a subjective criterion has been conducted. A group of 4 people (not including the authors) were charged of the task of selecting the visually more representative frames in each shot, and results of human analysis were compared with the output of the r-frame selector. For the sake of simplicity, the shot test set was made up by only a portion of the complete DB. In particular, the test set was composed by 60 shots, belonging to the following categories:

- Still shots.
- Shots with evident simple motion (zoom or pan).
- Shots with evident composite motion.

Observers were required to give an estimate of how many and which frames had to be considered as significant to represent the visual meaning of the shot in consideration. The results were similar to those obtained by using the r-frame extractor in over the 65 percent of cases, nearly touching the 94 percent for shots with simple motion. The tendency to oversampling was confirmed mainly in shots characterized by the presence of a moving object that maintains its global position with respect to a nearly fixed background (e.g., a news speaker moving hands). In such cases, perhaps, methods based on the similarity of color histograms should work better. Our technique is more effective for shots where homogeneous motion, e.g., pan or zoom, is dominant. In such cases, color-based techniques could fail to correctly detect r-frames in presence of a slowly varying color distribution.

4.3. Feature DB structure

The feature DB is structured in a hierarchical way. At the highest level is the video descriptor; this descriptor consists of:

- a pointer to the video in the raw-data DB,
- the video duration (in seconds),
- the number of shots contained in the video,
- a pointer to the shot descriptor for each shot belonging to the video.

The shot descriptor consists of:

- a pointer to the shot in the raw-data DB,
- the shot duration (in seconds),
- the number of r-frames contained in the shot,
- a pointer to the r-frame descriptor for each r-frame belonging to the shot.

The r-frame descriptor consists of attributes of both static and dynamic kind:

- a pointer to the r-frame in the raw-data DB,
- a pointer to the r-frame static descriptors,
- a pointer to the r-frame motion-based descriptor.

R-frames (or still images) are globally described. Static descriptors are based on texture and color. Motion-based descriptors are based on the optical flow field of the r-frame, and their computation involves considering a few frames after or before and after the r-frame. The logical structure of the feature DB is shown in figure 3.

4.4. Static descriptors

4.4.1. Color descriptors. Color is a very powerful feature in finding similar images. Even if textural, geometrical and motion features may be needed to perform effective queries and to eliminate false positive retrieval, it is believed that color indexing will retain its importance due to the fast processing of this kind of queries and to the simpleness in automatically computing color features from raw data. In the last years several color based techniques have been proposed for video annotation [5, 13, 32, 44, 48, 49, 58].

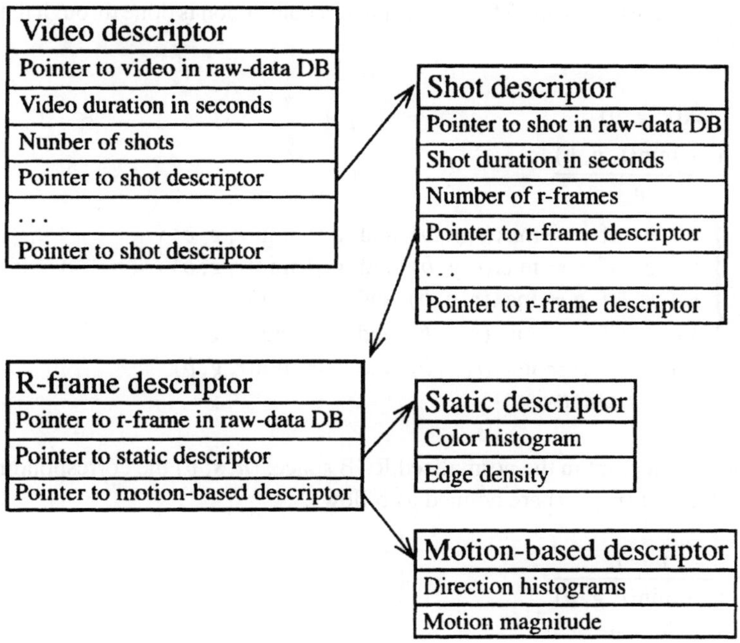

Figure 3. Logical structure of the feature DB.

There are two main classes of color indexing techniques: those based on global color distributions and those based on local color features. Other slightly different approaches to color indexing appeared in the last year [44, 47].

In the QBIC system [13, 32] color based feature extraction is done through color space conversion, quantization and clustering. In this way a $K \times 1$ vector is obtained for each image, where K is the number of *super-cells*, i.e., partitions of the color space. To compute image similarity a L_2 related metric is used.

In [48], the authors propose a technique that allows for a reduction of space required to characterize each image and improve searching speed. They avoid the large requirement of storing the whole color histogram and propose a set of just nine color moments (three per channel) to describe an image and a metric to compare these features.

Zhang et al. [58] use techniques similar to both of the above mentioned, moreover they use dominant colors and mean-brightness. In comparing two images different metrics are used for different features.

In [5] Ardizzone et al. propose a simple but effective method based on a 3-dimensional quantized color histogram in the RGB space and a quadratic distance metric.

A different approach is presented in [44], where the authors propose a method based on *color sets* that allows for querying by color regions, so avoiding the segmentation step.

In the current implementation of JACOB we use a quantized histogram in the HSV color space and an Euclidean metric to compare the query image to images contained in the database.

Since input images are in the RGB color space, a conversion is done through the following equations [20]:

$$v = \max(r, g, b)$$
$$s = \frac{v - \min(r, g, b)}{v}$$
$$h = \begin{cases} 5 + \acute{b} & \text{if } r = \max(r, g, b) \text{ and } g = \min(r, g, b) \\ 1 - \acute{g} & \text{if } r = \max(r, g, b) \text{ and } g \neq \min(r, g, b) \\ 1 + \acute{r} & \text{if } g = \max(r, g, b) \text{ and } b = \min(r, g, b) \\ 3 - \acute{b} & \text{if } g = \max(r, g, b) \text{ and } b \neq \min(r, g, b) \\ 3 + \acute{g} & \text{if } b = \max(r, g, b) \text{ and } r = \min(r, g, b) \\ 5 - \acute{r} & \text{otherwise} \end{cases}$$

where (r, g, b) is a point in the normalized RGB space, (h, s, v) the corresponding point in the HSV space and $(\acute{r}, \acute{g}, \acute{b})$ are defined as follows:

$$\acute{r} = \frac{v - r}{v - \min(r, g, b)}$$
$$\acute{g} = \frac{v - g}{v - \min(r, g, b)}$$
$$\acute{b} = \frac{v - b}{v - \min(r, g, b)}$$

For $r, g, b \in [0 \cdots 1]$, the conversion gives $h \in [0 \cdots 6]$, and $s, v \in [0 \cdots 1]$.

The color space quantization needed to compute a discrete color histogram is done using a technique similar to that proposed in [44].

In more detail we compute the quantized HSV histogram in the following way:

$$H(h, s, v) = p((h * 6/Q_h) \leq x_h < ((h + 1) * 6/Q_h) \mid (s/Q_s) \leq x_s < ((s + 1)/Q_s) \mid (v/Q_v) \leq x_v < ((v + 1)/Q_v)) \quad (1)$$

where Q_h, Q_s and Q_v are the quantization steps respectively used for h, s and v; $h = 0, 1, \ldots, Q_h - 1, s = 0, 1, \ldots, Q_s - 1, v = 0, 1, \ldots, Q_v - 1$; $H(h, s, v)$ is the joint probability that a generic pixels $\mathbf{x} = (x_h, x_s, x_v)^T$ belonging to the r-frame has a color value (h, s, v) in the quantized color space.

Believing that hue is the perceptually more significant feature, we use a finest quantization for it. In particular we put $Q_h = 18$ corresponding to a step every 20°, $Q_s = Q_v = 3$. In such a way we obtain a 162 bins histogram $(18 \times 3 \times 3 = 162)$.

It is convenient to reduce the three-dimensional histogram to a single variable histogram, to this aim we perform the following transformation:

$$l = hQ_sQ_v + sQ_v + v; \quad (2)$$

with $l = 0, 1, \ldots, Q_h Q_s Q_v - 1$; in our case $l = 0, 1, \ldots, 161$. The color histograms may be now represented by a 162×1 vector. Color histograms of different images are compared using the Euclidean distance.

We use this feature vector and the Euclidean distance because they outperform other implemented techniques. In particular we compared our results with the ones obtained by Stricker and Orengo [48] and by ourselves [23]. In [48] the color index contains only dominant features, expressed by the first three moments of each color channel of the HSV image. In [23] we applied the technique of histogram quantization with L_2 distance directly to RGB images. Our implementation of [48] is based on the above mentioned quantization of the HSV color space; the weight matrix we used in our experiments is the same used in [47]. Experimental results of these different methods will be compared in the next section.

4.4.2. Texture descriptors. Texture content of an image is a fundamental feature in classification and recognition problems. Due to its potential importance in content-based retrieval and querying by example texture features have been vastly investigated.

Several texture descriptors have been proposed that try to mimic the human similarity concept [27, 38, 39, 50]. However the texture features proposed are useful only in classifying homogeneous texture. Generic images usually contain different kinds of texture, so that a global texture descriptor hardly may describe the content of the whole image.

Tamura et al. [50] proposed six texture descriptors, namely, *coarseness*, *contrast*, *directionality*, *linelikeness*, *regularity* and *roughness*; Liu and Picard [27] proposed other features that result very effective in discrimination and classification of homogeneous texture. Anyway this features are useless if computed for non-segmented images.

The texture features we use in JACOB are related to coarseness, directionality and position of texture within the image.

All these features are based on edge density measures. Edge density is directly related to coarseness, directionality is addressed by repeating the edge measure for different directions and spatial position is taken into account by a simple partitioning of the r-frame.

In particular, we first subdivide the r-frame into four equal regions. For each region we compute the edge maps through directional masks respectively aligned along the directions $0°, 45°, 90°$ and $135°$. Values of edge map exceeding a fixed threshold are considered edge pixels. The threshold value has been determined experimentally.

The ratio between the number of edge pixels and the total number of pixels is the edge density. Since we determine 4 edge density values for each region, we have a 16×1 texture-based vector.

Other texture descriptors used in content-based retrieval [23] in spite of their computational cost are not so descriptive as the above mentioned or require an a priori image segmentation. Some edge maps are reported in figure 4.

Another technique able to describe the texture content is under development at our lab. It consists of a texture-based image segmentation allowing the detection of the largest region in the image; this region is assumed to have a dominant texture, i.e., the texture feature that will be used to characterize the whole image. For this approach texture descriptors like the ones proposed in [27] will probably perform better than edge density.

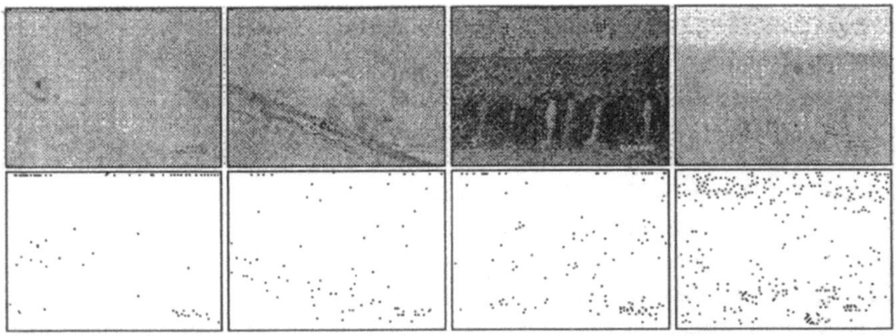

(a)

(b)

Figure 4. Edge maps of images with low (a) and high (b) edge density.

4.5. Motion based descriptor

Motion-based descriptors are based on the optical flow field [19] of the r-frame, and their computation involves considering a few frames after or before and after the r-frame. We used the Nagel [30, 31] technique as implemented in [8]. Essentially this is a gradient-based technique and uses the second-order derivatives to measure optical flow. The basic measurements are integrated using a global smoothness constraint. The problem is formulated as the minimization of the functional:

$$\iint (\nabla I^T \mathbf{v} + I_t)^2 + \frac{\alpha^2}{\|\nabla I\|_2^2 + 2\delta} \times \left[(u_x I_y - u_y I_x)^2 + (v_x I_y - v_y I_x)^2 + \delta\left(u_x^2 + u_y^2 + v_x^2 + v_y^2\right)\right] dx\, dy \tag{3}$$

where $I(\mathbf{x}, t)$ is the intensity of the pixel at location $\mathbf{x} = (x, y)^T$ and time t, $\mathbf{v} = (u, v)^T$ is the optical flow, $I_t, I_x, I_y, u_x, u_y, v_x, v_y$ are the partial derivative of I, u, v with respect to t, x, y, $\nabla I = (I_x(\mathbf{x}, t), I_y(\mathbf{x}, t))^T$ and α, δ are numerical constants. With the use of Gauss-Seidel iterations, the solution may be expressed in an iterative form. Details on this technique and its implementation can be found in [8].

In our implementation the flow field is then truncated and normalized (values of $M(x, y) \geq 10$ are put to 10; then $M(x, y) \to M(x, y)/10$; where $M(x, y)$ is the flow vector magnitude expressed in pixels) so that all the vectors in the flow field have magnitude in the range (0–1). This technique allows to obtain a dense and sufficiently precise flow field at a reasonable computational cost.

Once the optical flow field is computed, we need a method able to code the associated information in a form adequate for content-based querying. First we segment the flow field into four equal region; for each region we then compute motion based features. The splitting was performed to preserve spatially related information that are not integrated in the computed features.

The motion features are the following:

$$\mu = \frac{1}{L_x L_y} \sum_{x=0}^{L_x-1} \sum_{y=0}^{L_y-1} M(x, y) \tag{4}$$

$$H(\theta) = \frac{1}{\mu} \sum_{x=0}^{L_x-1} \sum_{y=0}^{L_y-1} M(x, y)\, \psi(\alpha(x, y), \theta, \Delta\theta) \tag{5}$$

where $M(x, y)$ and $\alpha(x, y)$ are respectively the magnitude and the phase of the normalized flow field vector at (x, y), the integrals are computed over the whole region and ψ is the function:

$$\psi(\alpha, \theta, \Delta\theta) = \begin{cases} 1 & \text{when } \left(\theta - \frac{\Delta\theta}{2}\right) \leq \alpha < \left(\theta + \frac{\Delta\theta}{2}\right) \\ 0 & \text{otherwise} \end{cases} \tag{6}$$

These features may be interpreted in the following way: μ is a measure of the average motion magnitude in the considered region, while $H(\theta)$ is a sort of normalized histogram of motion vectors directions. In our implementation we used $\Delta\theta = 10^\circ$.

5. DB querying

5.1. *Query processing*

Queries may be either direct or by example. To perform a direct query the user has to insert a few values representing the color histogram and/or the texture features and/or the motion based features. Queries may be based on one or more of the above mentioned features and the user can specify the relative weight of various features.

Using such a query, an user could, for example, search for a shot of people playing soccer by specifying the dominant color (green); to restrict the query he or she could also specify the image coarseness (low in this case). In another case the user could search for the videos with a news speaker; in such a situation the user could make the query more precise by using the motion descriptors (low-motion in this case). Once retrieved one or more shots similar to the one searched, the user could refine his query using one of the retrieved shots as the seed for a successive query by example.

In processing a query by example, the system computes the static feature vectors of the query image and compares them with the feature vectors pre-stored in the feature DB. Motion based features are optionally specified by the user in a direct way. Direct queries are performed building a feature vector by the user provided values and comparing it with the feature vectors pre-stored in the feature DB. Queries (direct or by example) are performed through a sequential scan in the feature DB; similarity among images is evaluated by using different metrics for different features. The importance of different features is established taking into account the statistics of the database and the user provided weights, as it will be shown in what follows.

5.2. *Multifeature querying*

When performing multifeature queries, the user chooses a value between 0 and 1 to assess the importance of a feature with respect to another one. Moreover, a method to adequately weight the distances computed for each feature descriptor (color, texture, motion) is needed to obtain a global similarity value. Otherwise, images with a similar color distribution could give a similarity value different from that one obtained from images with similar texture. The same holds when other features are considered. In conclusion a distance normalization is necessary before of the application of user provided weights.

An interesting approach based on the cooperation of models of different features (*the society of models*) has been proposed to solve this problem in [28, 37]. This approach has the main limitation in the need of rebuild all the underlying hierarchical data structure when a new image is added to the database.

In this paper we present an original method to adequately weight the distances computed for each feature descriptor. Our approach is based on a statistical analysis of feature distances.

In particular we compute a probability distribution for the metric associated to each feature, comparing every r-frame in the database (about 1500) with all the others. In this way we obtain a probability distribution for the dissimilarity measure related to each feature. These probability distributions are used to make all the distances fit the range $[0 \cdots 1]$. The underlying assumption is that images currently contained in the database be representative of all images the system could contain also in the future.

The probability distributions for the features used in the current implementation of our system are reported in figure 5.

To rescale distances to the range $[0 \cdots 1]$ we use the following equation:

$$\tilde{d} = \begin{cases} 1 & \text{if } d > d_m \\ \dfrac{d}{d_m} & \text{otherwise} \end{cases} \tag{7}$$

where d is the distance to be normalized, $\tilde{d}$ is the normalized distance and d_m is the distance corresponding to the maximum of the probability distribution.

Once this normalization step has been performed on all the distances, a global dissimilarity measure can be computed in the following way:

$$d(\mathbf{x}, \mathbf{y}) = \sum_{i=1}^{F} w_i \tilde{d}_i(\mathbf{x}, \mathbf{y}) \tag{8}$$

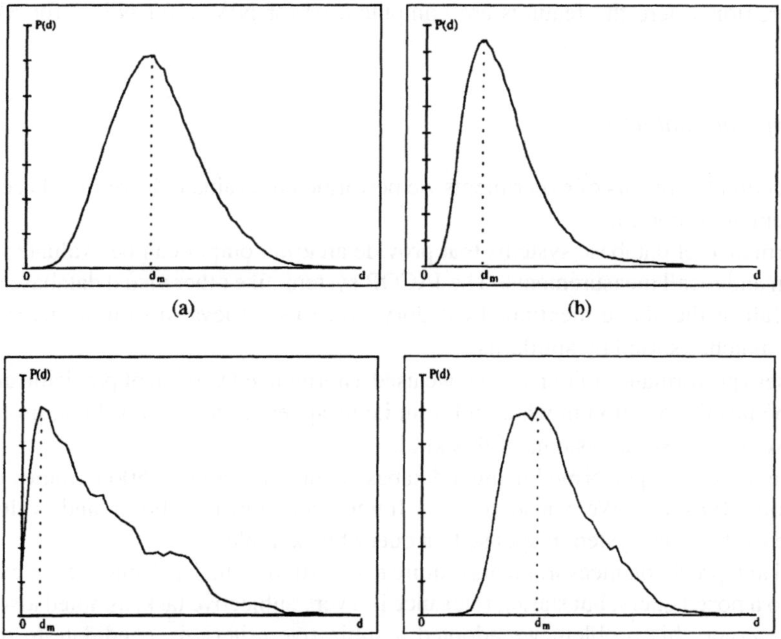

Figure 5. Probability distributions related to the used metrics: (a) Euclidean distance between HSV histograms, (b) Euclidean distance between texture features, (c) Euclidean distance between motion magnitudes, (d) Euclidean distance between motion direction histograms.

where w_i is the weight (in the range $[0 \cdots 1]$) the user wants to assign to the ith feature, F is the number of features used (in our case $f = 4$) and $\tilde{d}_i(\mathbf{x}, \mathbf{y})$ is the normalized distance, related to the ith feature, between the images whose feature vectors are respectively $\mathbf{x}$ and $\mathbf{y}$.

A feature vector $\mathbf{x}$ is composed of four subvectors containing respectively the HSV color histogram, the edge density vectors, the motion magnitude values and the motion direction histograms:

$$\mathbf{x} = [\mathbf{x}_c \ \mathbf{x}_t \ \mathbf{x}_{\text{mm}} \ \mathbf{x}_{\text{md}}]^T \tag{9}$$

where:

$$\mathbf{x}_t = \begin{bmatrix} \mathbf{x}_{t,0} & \mathbf{x}_{t,1} \\ \mathbf{x}_{t,2} & \mathbf{x}_{t,3} \end{bmatrix}, \ \mathbf{x}_{\text{mm}} = \begin{bmatrix} x_{\text{mm},0} & x_{\text{mm},1} \\ x_{\text{mm},2} & x_{\text{mm},3} \end{bmatrix}, \ \mathbf{x}_{\text{md}} = \begin{bmatrix} \mathbf{x}_{\text{md},0} & \mathbf{x}_{\text{md},1} \\ \mathbf{x}_{\text{md},2} & \mathbf{x}_{\text{md},3} \end{bmatrix} \tag{10}$$

In particular $\mathbf{x}_c$ is the 162 bins quantized HSV color histogram, $\mathbf{x}_{t,i}$ are the vectors containing the edge density along the main four directions, $x_{\text{mm},i}$ are the average motion magnitude values and $\mathbf{x}_{\text{md},i}$ are the 36 bins motion direction histograms; i indicates the r-frame region where the features are computed, (0 for NW, 1 for NE, 2 for SW, 3 for SE).

5.3. *Experimental results*

In this section the results of experiments we performed to evaluate the retrieval accuracy of our system are reported.

Performance of database systems that provide an *exact* output can be evaluated through precision and recall measurements. The JACOB system, like other visual database systems, doesn't fall in the above mentioned category, since its retrieval operation gives a list of possible matches sorted by similarity.

To assess performance of our system we used a normalized version of precision and recall that embodies the position in which relevant items appear in the retrieval list, proposed by Faloutsos et al. [13] for systems of this kind.

All the tests were performed using a database containing about 1500 r-frames obtained from about 500 shots. We considered 20 r-frames randomically chosen and evaluated for each one of them the system response to a query by example.

Recall and precision measurements require to determine which r-frames are relevant with respect to a posed query, but stating relevance is a very subjective task, as noted also in [36].

To overcome this problem we adopted a subjective criterion: candidate-to-relevance r-frames for each query were determined by four different people (not including the authors) and a r-frame was considered as relevant if at least three people chose it.

Once known the *correct* query result we are able to evaluate system performances. Fixed to n the number of images to be retrieved, for each query we performed the following measures:

- AVRR the average rank of all relevant, retrieved images
- IAVRR the ideal average rank, i.e., when all the relevant images are ranked at the top
- MT the number of relevant images that were missed
- AVRR/IAVRR.

We used the following definitions:

$$\mathrm{AVRR} = \frac{1}{R}\sum_{r=1}^{R} \rho_r$$

$$\mathrm{IAVRR} = \frac{T}{2}$$

$$\mathrm{MT} = \frac{R}{T}$$

where R is the number of relevant images among the n retrieved, ρ_r is the rank of the rth relevant retrieved image and T is the total number of images relevant to the posed query.

Note that these measures depend on n, the number of retrieved images. In our experiments we performed each query twice, one for $n = 32$ and one for $n = 64$.

In what follows we report detailed results for a few queries and average values for all the test queries. Several color similarity methods were used, so results of different kinds of query by color are also reported.

Detailed results are reported for queries related to the following r-frames:

1. waterpolo (7 relevant r-frames)
2. interview (5 relevant r-frames)
3. TV-show (16 relevant r-frames)
4. TV-movie (12 relevant r-frames)
5. cycling race (14 relevant r-frames)

In Tables 1 and 2 the numerical results of color based queries are reported, respectively for $n = 32$ and $n = 64$. Tables 3 and 4 summarize the results of texture based queries for $n = 32$ and $n = 64$.

Results show that color indexing exhibits a behavior decisely good, with the exception of query 5. This is probably due to the fact that the frames belonging to the cluster related

Table 1. Results of queries by color for the five test images (see text) with $n = 32$.

	Query 1	Query 2	Query 3	Query 4	Query 5
AVRR	5.00	3.40	11.21	6.27	10.62
IAVRR	3.50	2.50	8.00	6.00	7.00
AVRR/IAVRR	1.43	1.36	1.40	1.04	1.52
MT	1.00	1.00	0.87	0.92	0.57

Table 2. Results of queries by color for the five test images (see text) with $n = 64$.

	Query 1	Query 2	Query 3	Query 4	Query 5
AVRR	5.00	3.40	16.94	6.27	16.00
IAVRR	3.50	2.50	8.00	6.00	7.00
AVRR/IAVRR	1.43	1.36	2.12	1.04	2.28
MT	1.00	1.00	1.00	0.92	0.64

Table 3. Results of queries by texture for five test images (see text) with $n = 32$.

	Query 1	Query 2	Query 3	Query 4	Query 5
AVRR	8.58	12.27	15.03	13.19	7.88
IAVRR	12.50	10.50	10.00	11.50	8.50
AVRR/IAVRR	0.69	1.17	1.50	1.15	0.93
MT	0.48	0.52	0.44	0.62	0.39

Table 4. Results of queries by texture for five test images (see text) with $n = 64$.

	Query 1	Query 2	Query 3	Query 4	Query 5
AVRR	20.88	16.69	17.34	13.19	14.28
IAVRR	12.50	10.50	10.00	11.50	8.50
AVRR/IAVRR	1.67	1.59	1.73	1.15	1.68
MT	0.68	0.62	0.52	0.62	0.46

to this query image present a scarcely marked hue. Results of texture queries are by far less encouraging. This is probably due to the missing segmentation step and to the weakness of the used texture features.

To evaluate queries by motion we need a set of shots relevant with respect to the posed query. Finding this kind of relevance is a problem not so simple as for static images; browsing through over 500 shots to detect which of them are relevant with respect to motion magnitude or motion direction is not possible.

To partially overcome this difficulty we evaluated how many retrieved shots are relevant after a direct query has been posed. In this way the only measurement we can perform is the AVRR that in this case is something like precision, but we have no information about recall.

A similar criterion has been adopted to assess the effectiveness of multifeature queries that embody motion features.

Tables and 5 and 6 show results of queries by motion magnitude and motion direction. In both cases $n = 32$. In these tables we report only the number of relevant retrieved (in the sense above mentioned) and AVRR.

Finally, the average values of AVRR, IAVRR, AVRR/IAVRR and MT related to all 20 test queries are reported in Tables 7 and 8, respectively for $n = 32$ and $n = 64$.

In Table 9 results are reported relative to multifeature querying. The test queries are the same used in the other experiments (waterpolo, interview, etc...). The relevant r-frames for each query are the same that were considered for color and texture based experiments and that, at the same time, satisfy to a given motion constraint. For example, Query 1 is now

Table 5. Results of queries by motion magnitude for five test queries (see text) with $n = 32$.

	Query 1	Query 2	Query 3	Query 4	Query 5
R	22	23	24	18	22
AVRR	15.14	15.48	14.92	13.24	14.98

Table 6. Results of queries by motion direction for five test queries (see text) with $n = 32$.

	Query 1	Query 2	Query 3	Query 4	Query 5
R	20	22	25	19	20
AVRR	16.60	15.59	15.12	14.01	15.25

Table 7. Average query results for twenty test queries by color, texture, motion magnitude and motion direction ($n = 32$).

	Color	Texture	Magnitude	Direction
AVRR	6.93	11.12	14.62	15.26
IAVRR	5.50	10.83	n.a.	n.a.
AVRR/IAVRR	1.27	1.06	n.a.	n.a.
MT	0.85	0.47	n.a.	n.a.

Table 8. Average query results for twenty test queries by color and texture ($n = 64$).

	Color	Texture
AVRR	10.07	21.99
IAVRR	5.50	10.83
AVRR/IAVRR	1.73	2.08
MT	0.91	0.70

Table 9. Multifeature querying results ($n = 32$).

	Query 1	Query 2	Query 3	Query 4	Query 5
AVRR	3.66	3.80	9.70	7.37	10.00
IAVRR	1.50	2.50	5.00	4.00	5.00
AVRR/IAVRR	2.44	1.52	1.94	1.84	2.00
MT	1.00	1.00	1.00	1.00	0.60

restricted to waterpolo (mainly blue and fine textured) left-panning shots. Moreover queries were executed giving the same weight to color and feature. Results are very encouraging as motion constraints exhibit high discriminant power in most cases; best results were obtained in shots containing homogeneous or slow motion. Obviously the worst results are relative to heterogeneous shots, i.e., shots containing several moving object. Finally, it should be noted that the results of multifeature queries are slightly better than only color queries, due to the indexing contribution by other descriptors.

Table 10 reports the results of color based queries for three kinds of descriptors. As mentioned in the previous subsection 4.4.1, beside the HSV histograms with L_2 distance we also indexed r-frames by using RGB histograms with L_2 distance and HSV moments as defined in [48]. Experimental results clearly assert the superiority of the HSV L_2 technique as far as the retrieval capabilities are concerned, so that we embodied it in the current implementation of JACOB, despite of its more heavy computational load.

The current system, running on a 200 MHz SGI workstation, performs real-time querying on our database containing about 1500 r-frames; as the response time scales linearly with the number of r-frames we expect that a system based on such an indexing scheme could

Table 10. Sample query by color results using different color similarity measures ($n = 64$).

	RGB L_2	HSV L_2	HSV moments
AVRR	12.03	6.93	11.51
IAVRR	5.50	5.50	5.50
AVRR/IAVRR	2.59	1.27	1.77
MT	0.84	0.85	0.55

Figure 6. Query by example results. On the top-left is the query image *waterpolo*, the others are the r-frames retrieved in decreasing similarity order for $n = 32$. Only color information was used. The results would be more expressive if looking at the color versions.

operate in interactive-time only if containing no more than 10–20,000 r-frames. For larger database an optimized indexing scheme will be needed.

To give a more complete idea of the behavior of JACOB, in the following some other test queries are further described. The three queries by example shown in figures 6, 7 and 8 use the same query image (waterpolo) but different values for color and texture importance; in particular the shown results refer to querying by example, using only color information, using only texture information and using both color and texture information.

The results of two motion based queries are reported in figure 9; the former is related to a direct query for r-frames with a low motion magnitude, while the latter is related to a query looking for r-frames with a high motion magnitude. As shown by this example, motion

Figure 7. Query by example results. On the top-left is the query image *waterpolo*, the others are the r-frames retrieved in decreasing similarity order for $n = 32$. Only color information was used.

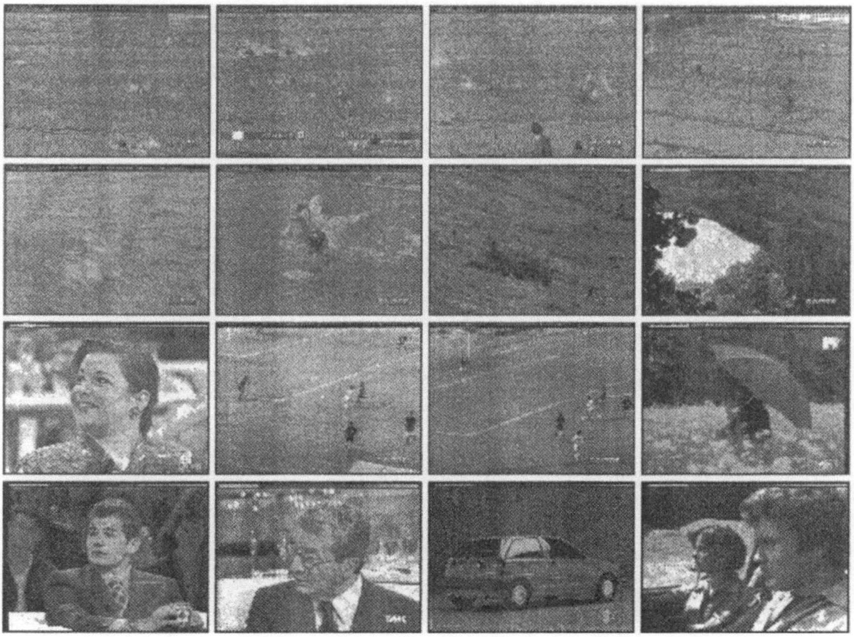

Figure 8. Query by example results. On the top-left is the query image *waterpolo*, the others are the r-frames retrieved in decreasing similarity order. Color and texture information was used with equal weight. The results would be more expressive if looking at the color versions.

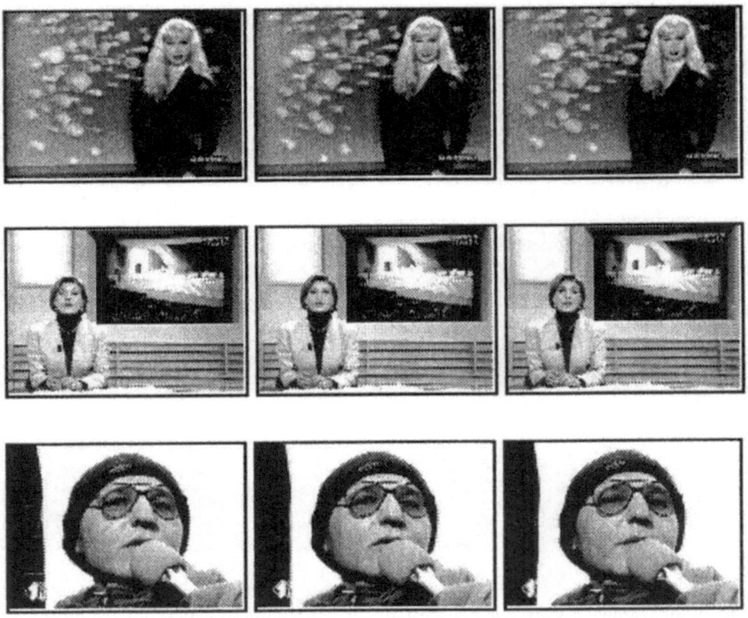

(a)

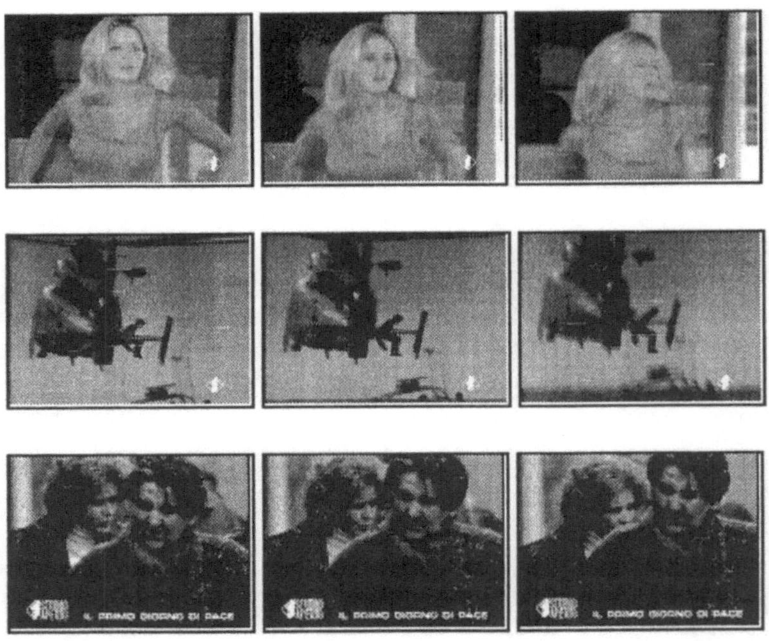

(b)

Figure 9. Motion-based queries: (a) queries for low motion, (b) queries for high motion. The r-frames are reported in the middle with their adjacent frames to evidentiate the instantaneous motion.

based queries may result very useful in discriminating among classes of r-frames in large databases.

6. Concluding remarks

In this paper we described a system using video content for annotation and retrieval. The major characteristics of the system are the automatic indexing capability (no human action is required during the DB population step) and the domain independence.

The system uses color, texture and motion features. These features are currently related to entire images. Better results may be certainly obtained using single object's descriptors. To this aim a segmentation step is needed to locate moving objects and discriminate them from the background. Obtaining robust and automatic segmentation algorithms has been proved to be a very difficult task on static images. Information associated to object motion may play a crucial role in solving this problem. With this in the mind, we are now exploring the feasibility of automatic and semi-automatic image segmentation tools.

Another improvement to our system may become by the integration of textual information on the video typology (i.e., sport, film, news, etc...) with the automatically computed features. This information, although manually inserted by the operator, could dramatically improve the system performance during retrieval. Other areas of future works include optimized database accesses, a more powerful and friendly user interface, the definition of an appropriate query language and the formalization of the data model.

The system was developed in C and X11 on a DEC AXP3000 workstation; the WWW demo was developed and still runs on a DECstation 5000; the tests were performed on a 200 MHz SGI Indigo2 workstation.

Note

1. Also named key-frames by several authors; here we adopt the terminology used in [14] and elsewhere.

References

1. P. Aigrain and P. Joly, "Medium knowledge-based macro-segmentation of video into sequences," in Intelligent Multimedia Information Retrieval, M. Maybury (Ed.), 1996.
2. E. Ardizzone and M. La Cascia, "Motion labeling in video databases," Journal of Visual Languages and Computing: Special Issue on Image and Video Database Visual Browsing Querying and Retrieval, 1996, (submitted).
3. E. Ardizzone, A. Chella, and S. Gaglio, "A hybrid architecture for shape reconstruction and object recognition," in International Journal of Intelligent Systems, 1996, (in press).
4. E. Ardizzone, G.A.M. Gioiello, M. La Cascia, and D. Molinelli, "A real-time neural approach to scene cut detection," in Proc. of IS&T/SPIE—Storage & Retrieval for Image and Video Databases IV, San Jose, 1996.
5. E. Ardizzone, M. La Cascia, and D. Molinelli, "Motion and color based video indexing and retrieval," in Proc. of Int. Conf. on Pattern Recognition, ICPR, Wien, Austria, 1996.
6. F. Arman, A. Hsu, and M.Y. Chiu, "Image processing on compressed data for large video databases," in Proc. First ACM Int. Conf. Multimedia, 1993.
7. J.R. Bach, S. Paul, and R. Jain, "A visual information management system for the interactive retrieval of faces," IEEE Transaction on Knowledge and Data Engineering, Vol. 5, 1993.

8. J.L. Barron, D.J. Fleet, and S.S. Beauchemin, "Performances of optical flow techniques," Int. Journal of Computer Vision, Vol. 12, p. 43, 1994.
9. M.G. Christel, "Addressing the contents of video in a digital library," in Proc. of ACM Workshop on Effective Abstractions in Multimedia: Layout, Presentation and Interaction, San Francisco, 1995.
10. J.M. Corridoni and A. DelBimbo, "Automatic video segmentation through editing analysis," in Proc. of 8th Int. Conf. on Image Analysis and Processing, ICIAP, Sanremo, Italy, 1995.
11. J.M. Corridoni and A. DelBimbo, "Film semantic analysis," in Proc. of Computer Architecture for Machine Perception, CAMP, Como, Italy, 1995.
12. J.M. Corridoni, A. DelBimbo, and D. Lucarella, "Navigation and visualization of movies content," in Proc. Int. Conf. on Visual Languages, VL'95, Darmstadt, Germany, 1995.
13. C. Faloutsos, R. Barber, M. Flickner, J. Hafner, W. Niblack, D. Pektovic, and W. Equitz, "Efficient and effective querying by image content," Journal of Intelligent Information Systems, Vol. 3, p. 231, 1994.
14. M. Flickner et al. "Query by image and video content: The qbic system," IEEE Computer, Sept. 1995.
15. W.I. Grosky, "Multimedia information systems," IEEE Multimedia, Vol. 2, 1994.
16. V.N. Guditava and V.V. Raghavan, "Content-based image retrieval systems," IEEE Computer, Sept. 1995.
17. A. Hampapur, T. Weymouth, and R. Jain, "Digital video segmentation," in ACM Multimedia'94 Proceedings, ACM Press, 1994.
18. A. Hampapur, R. Jain, and T. Weymouth, "Production model based digital video segmentation," Journal of Multimedia Tools and Applications, Vol. 1, No. 1, pp. 9–46, March 1995.
19. B.K.P. Horn and B.G. Schunk, "Determining optical flow," Artificial Intelligence, p. 17, 1981.
20. R.W.G. Hunt, Measuring Color, John Wiley & Sons, 1989.
21. P.M. Kelly and T.M. Cannon, "Candid: Comparison algorithm for navigating digital image databases," in Proc. of the Seventh International Working Conference on Scientific and Statistical Database Management, Charlottesville VA, 1994.
22. P.M. Kelly, T.M. Cannon, and D.R. Hush, "Query by image example: The candid approach," in Proc. of SPIE: Storage and Retrieval for Image and Video Database III, 1995.
23. M. La Cascia and E. Ardizzone, "Jacob: Just a content-based query system for video databases," in Proc. of IEEE Int. Conf. on Acoustics, Speech and Signal Processing, ICASSP-96, Atlanta, May, 1996, pp. 7–10.
24. D. Lee, R. Barber, W. Niblack, M. Flickner, J. Hafner, and D. Petkovic, "Indexing for complex queries on a query by content image database," in Proceedings of the ICPR, Vol. 1, pp. 142–146, 1994.
25. D. Lee, R. Barber, W. Niblack, M. Flickner, J. Hafner, and D. Petkovic, "Query by image content using multiple objects and multiple features: User interface issue," in Proceeding of the ICIP, 1994.
26. W. Li, S. Gauch, J. Gauch, and K.M. Pua, "Vision: A digital video library," in ACM Digital Libraries, Bethseda, MD, 1996.
27. F. Liu and R.W. Picard, "Periodocity, directionality and randomness," Technical Report TR-320, MIT Media Lab.
28. T.P. Minka and R.W. Picard, "Interactive learning using a society of models," Technical Report TR-349, MIT Media Lab.
29. A. Nagasaka and Y. Tanaka, "Automatic video indexing and full-motion search for object appearances," in Proc. IFIP TC2/WG2.6 Second Working Conference on Visual Database System, 1991.
30. H.H. Nagel, "Displacement vectors derived from second-orderintensity variations in image sequences," Computer Vision, Graphics, Image Processing, Vol. 21, 1983.
31. H.H. Nagel, "On the estimation of optical flow: Relations between different approaches and some new results," Artificial Intelligence, Vol. 33, 1987.
32. W. Niblack et al., "The qbic project: Querying images by content using color, texture and shape," in IS&T/SPIE Symposium on Electronic Imaging: Science and Technology—Storage & Retrieval for Image and Video Databases I, San Jose, CA, 1993.
33. V.E. Ogle and M. Stonebraker, "Chabot: Retrieval from a relational database of images," IEEE Computer, Sept. 1995.

34. E. Oomoto and K. Tanaka, "Ovid: Design and implementation of a video-object database system," IEEE Transaction on Knowledge and Data Engineering, Vol. 5, Aug. 1994.
35. A. Pentland, R.W. Picard, and S. Sclaroff, "Photobook: Tools for content-based manipulation of image databases," in Proc. of SPIE: Storage and Retrieval Image and Video Database II, San Jose, Feb. 6–10, 1994.
36. R.W. Picard, "Computer learning of subjectivity," Technical Report TR-359, MIT Media Lab.
37. R.W. Picard, "Toward a visual thesaurus," in Proc. of Springer Werlag Workshops in Computing, MIRO, Glasgow, 1995.
38. R.W. Picard and T. Kabir, "Finding similar patterns in large image databases," in Proc. of IEEE Int. Conf. on Acoustics, Speech and Signal Processing, ICASSP, Minneapolis, MN, 1993.
39. R.W. Picard, T. Kabir, and F. Liu, "Real-time recognition with the entire broadatz texture database," in Proc. of IEEE Int. Conf. on Computer Vision and Pattern Recognition, CVPR, New York, NY. 1993.
40. R.W. Picard and T.P. Minka, "Vision texture for annotation," Technical Report TR-302, MIT Media Lab.
41. M.J.D. Powell, "Restart procedures for the conjugate gradient method," Mathematical Programming, Vol. 12, pp. 241–254, 1968.
42. S. Sclaroff, "Deformable prototypes for encoding shape categories in image databases," Pattern Recognition: Special issue on image databases, 1996, (to appear).
43. J.R. Smith and S.-F. Chang, "Querying by color regions using the visualseek content-based visual query system," in Intelligent Multimedia Information Retrieval, M. Maybury (Ed.), 1996.
44. J.R. Smith and S.-F. Chang, "Tools and techniques for color image retrieval," in Proc. of IS&T SPIE: Storage and Retrieval Image and Video Database IV, San Jose, CA, 1996.
45. R.K. Srihari, "Automatic indexing and content-based retrieval of captioned images," IEEE Computer, Sept. 1995.
46. H.S. Stone and T.G. Shamoon, "The use of image content to control image retrieval and image processing," Technical Report, Internal Report, NEC Research Institute, 1995.
47. M. Stricker and A. Dimai, "Color indexing with weak spatial constraints," in Proc. of IS&T SPIE: Storage and Retrieval Image and Video Database IV, San Jose, CA, 1996.
48. M. Stricker and M. Orengo, "Similarity of color images," in Proc. of IS&T SPIE: Storage and Retrieval Image and Video Database III, San Jose, CA, 1995.
49. M. Swain and D. Ballard, "Color indexing," Int. Journal of Computer Vision, Vol. 7, p. 11, 1991.
50. H. Tamura, S. Mori, and T. Yamawaki, "Textural features corresponding to visual perception," IEEE Transaction on Systems, Man and Cybernetics, Vol. 8, No. 6, 1978.
51. W. Wolf, "Key-frame selection by motion analysis," in Proc. of IEEE Int. Conf. on Acoustics, Speech and Signal Processing, ICASSP, Atlanta, May 7–10, 1996.
52. B.L. Yeo and B. Liu, "Rapid scene analysis on compressed video," IEEE Trans. on Circuits and Systems for Video Technology, Vol. 5, Dec. 1995.
53. M.M. Yeung and B. Liu, "Efficient matching and clustering of video shot," in Proc. of IEEE Int. Conf. on Image Processing, ICIP, Washington, DC, 1995.
54. M.M. Yeung, B.L. Yeo, and B. Liu, "Extracting story units from long programs for video browsing and navigation," in Proc. of Int. Conf. on Multimedia Computing and Systems, 1996.
55. M.M. Yeung, B.L. Yeo, W. Wolf, and B. Liu, "Video browsing using clustering and scene transitions on compressed sequences," in Proc. of IS&T/SPIE Multimedia Computing and Networking, 1995.
56. A. Yoshitaka, S. Kishida, M. Hirakawa, and T. Ichikawa, "Knowledge-assisted content-based retrieval for multimedia databases," IEEE Multimedia, Vol. 1, 1994.
57. H.J. Zhang, A. Kankanhalli, and S.W. Smoliar, "Automatic partitioning of full-motion video," Multimedia Systems, Vol. 1, 1993.
58. H.J. Zhang, C.Y. Low, S.W. Smoliar, and J.H. Wu, "Video parsing retrieval and browsing: An integrated and content-based solution," in Proc. ACM Multimedia'95, pp. 15–24.

Edoardo Ardizzone is an assistant professor at the Dipartimento di Ingegneria Elettrica, Universita' di Palermo (Italy). He was one of founders of the Lab of Computer Science and Artificial Intelligence of the Universita' di Palermo, where he is currently charged of the course of Theory and Technique of Image Processing. Edoardo Ardizzone is a member of the Italian Chapter of IAPR and a founder member of AI*IA (Italian Association for Artificial Intelligence). His current research interests are in the fields of image analysis, computer vision and content-based image and video databases.

Marco La Cascia received the Laurea degree in Ingegneria Elettronica from the Universita' di Palermo, Palermo (Italy) in 1994. Currently he is a Doctoral student at the Dipartimento di Ingegneria Elettrica, Universita' di Palermo. His current research interests are video analysis and content-based retrieval in video databases.

Multimedia Tools and Applications 4, 57–83 (1997)

The Application of Video Semantics and Theme Representation in Automated Video Editing

FRANK NACK fn@uk.ac.lancs.comp
ALAN PARKES app@uk.ac.lancs.comp
Computing Department, Lancaster University, Lancaster LA1 4YW, UK

Abstract. This paper considers the automated generation of humorous video sequences from arbitrary video material. We present a simplified model of the editing process. We then outline our approach to narrativity and visual humour, discuss the problems of context and shot-order in video and consider influences on the editing process. We describe the role of themes and semantic fields in the generation of content oriented video scenes. We then present the architecture of AUTEUR, an experimental system that embodies mechanisms to interpret, manipulate and generate video. An example of a humorous video sequence generated by AUTEUR is described.

Keywords: video editing, video semantics, video representation, video retrieval

1. Introduction

The power of video images lies in their close resemblance to reality. This distinguishes film from written or spoken language, which seldom achieve such a direct representation of the real world. With current rapid developments in Multimedia, the use of still and motion pictures in computer applications is increasing. However, as large amounts of video can now be stored, the need to define techniques for retrieving, rearranging and presenting video on the basis of its content becomes more pressing.

Our work addresses the automated editing of video to realise a thematic specification. The problem of how to edit particular video to realise a theme, or tell a story, is one that rarely has a single, unique solution. Moreover, while a given sequence may have the desired effect for one viewer, it may fail in this respect for another. Video editing is a creative process. Research has produced computer based environments to assist with the editing, annotation and retrieval of video (e.g., [7, 11, 19–21, 25, 31, 32, 34]). However, such research has yet to produce techniques to automatically assemble video sequences that realise a given theme.

Our work focuses on the definition of methods to perform automated editing of video based on its semantic and syntactic aspects and on the conceptual representation of thematic goals and narrative. To reduce the complexity of this open-ended research program, we have set ourselves the initial goal of producing short sequences of video that realise the theme of *humour*. As will be seen, our approach draws on theories of humour, and a model of film editing, and has resulted in a prototype system, AUTEUR, that has achieved a limited degree of success in producing humorous film sequences. Our system is far from complete, and it should be appreciated that what is being presented in this paper is but a small step toward the goal of intelligent video editing systems.

The structure of the paper is as follows. We first present a simplified model of the editing process. We then discuss the semiotic, semantic, and syntactic dimensions of film, and their relevance to the enterprise of film editing. Theories of humour are then discussed, which leads to a description of our strategies for producing humorous films. We then go on to describe our prototype system, AUTEUR, along with an example of how AUTEUR creates a humorous film sequence. Finally, we assess our achievements thus far, and provide an overview of further work.

Please note that we use the terms *video* and *film* synonymously, and that we do not consider sound at this point in our research.

2. A model of film editing

The video editor has two key aims. First, he or she must arrange the material so that the resulting film becomes perceptible in its entirety, or the illusion of reality will be lost. Second, he or she must ensure that the intended theme engages the spectator both emotionally and intellectually. In this section, we describe a model of the video editing process which supports these aims. Our model is based on observations of video editors in their own environment.

In order to perform the required task, the editor must be equipped with knowledge *about* the target film, such as the topic, the story, the characters, the theme and the target audience. In the light of this knowledge, the editor first browses through the various available pieces of film so that they can be ordered and categorised. This usually results in shots and takes being placed on separate "heaps", each heap representing a potential scene. Each heap and its elements is annotated in a list which contains information such as heap identifier, shot identifier, shot length in frames and shot characteristics.

Examining the raw material usually evokes a chain of associations in the editor's mind. He or she recalls events, persons or emotions and these experiences may influence the created scene. At this stage the editor, the assistant and the director often talk more about their own experiences than about the actual material. These conversations often influence the refinement of the material to realise a given theme. In other words, those involved in the editing process are guided by their own experiences to a state of empathy with the target audience, as summarised in figure 1.

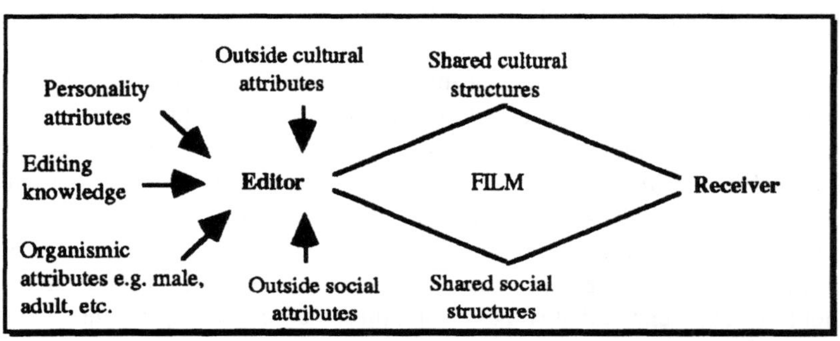

Figure 1. Influential communication factors (based on Tudor [33]).

Following the arrangement of the material into heaps, the refinement of scenes begins with a discussion of each scene with respect to the available material, its intention and its part in the overall story. Images make powerful visual statements, but narrative meaning arises from the specific interaction of shots, in terms of factors such as *length*, *rhythm*, *graphical direction*, *darkness and lightness* and *colour*. Every *cut* is intended to support both the conceptual content of the current scene, and the overall appearance of the film. Typical features of the editing process at this stage, which is known as the *rough cut*, are *insertion*, *elimination*, *substitution* or *permutation* of shots both within a scene, and the same for complete scenes within the overall structure of the film.

The rough cut stage leaves the film lacking a definite visual precision with respect to rhythm and technique, which it receives during the *fine cut*. The fine cut deals with the perceptually acceptable connection of two shots, which is determined partly by their graphical features (contour, centre of sight, shared axes, etc.). This stage of the editing process focuses on much smaller units of film (as small as one second in duration) than does the rough cut stage.

Figure 2 presents a simplified representation of the editing process, which serves as a basis for our prototype system. The model covers only the juxtaposition of takes, shots and scenes and does not consider editing for sound. Moreover, the model deals only with the rough cut stage.

However, the model serves as a workable approximation. It must be made clear that we are, at this stage, considering only the creation of a single scene where a start-shot is given. Thus, we focus on elements defined in figure 2 such as *information retrieval*, *scene creation*, *control effects* and *reordering* or *recreation* of scene structure. We exclude the creation of larger meaningful sequences of scenes.

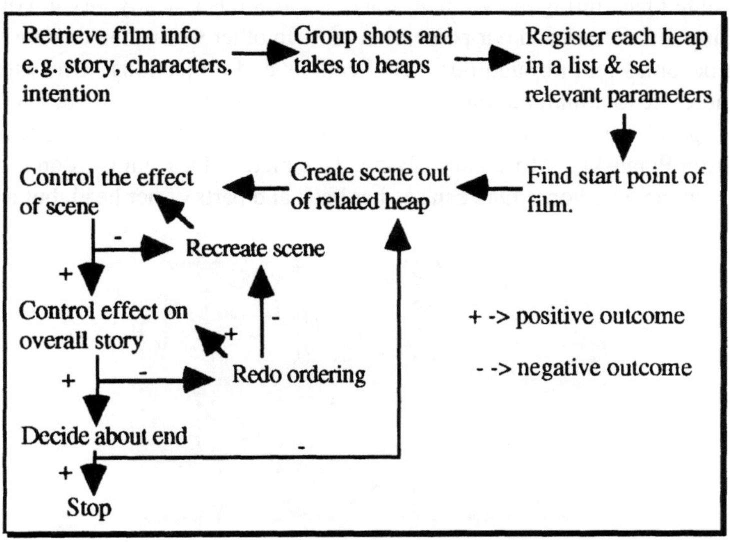

Figure 2. Simplified model of the film editing process.

3. The influence of visual form and function on film editing and perception

To portray a visual narrative, the visual material must be selected and arranged so that the intended theme can be appreciated by the spectator. A major problem, therefore, is to identify the structural relationship between film and story and specify how these are involved in leading the spectator to the intended interpretation.

3.1. Reality and imagination

Metz [17] develops the idea of *movement* as the main reason behind the psychological effect of reality within film. Unlike a photograph, which also represents reality in its objective reproduction of objects, film includes the element of motion, which is an almost totally *visual* experience (a counterexample from the real world is a bypassing train, which can also be detected audibly and haptically). The effect of motion cannot be reproduced unless one recreates the same order of reality, which means either giving the impression of reality or actually repeating reality itself.

Motion is clearly not the sole determinant of reality as represented in film. Film encourages us to suspend our belief that we are witnessing an artificially created world, because it confronts us with real people and objects. It could be argued that theatre achieves the same result. However, as Metz argues, theatre is not as convincing as film, because theatre is so obviously a part real life (in terms of social ritual, real actors, real stage, etc.). Though the actors in a play pretend to be in a different time and location, it is impossible for the spectator to accept the performance as reality because he or she shares the same space as the actors. For a film, on the other hand, there is no connection between the space of the spectator's reality and the space of the fictional film reality (e.g., Marlon Brando sitting in a Cambodian temple, during the Vietnam war). The result is a steady mixture of the reality of the ongoing film fiction and our perception of it. In other words, the denotative material of the film becomes real through our identifications and projections. One aspect of film reality is, therefore, our *imagination*, which means that film reality is created within us, the audience. A good example of the engagement of the film audience in the portrayed event is a scene from Polanski's "Rosemary's Baby" (see picture 1). Ruth Gordon is sitting on a bed, talking on the telephone. One can see her back and parts of her head, but not her face.

Picture 1. Ruth Gordon in Polanski's Rosemary's Baby (1968).

William A. Fraker, the film's cameraman, reported in an interview that he and Polanski actually observed members of the audience attempting to turn their heads to the right so that they could see around the wall and door frame to have a complete view of the character.

Thus, filmic reality is composed out of a number of elements which need to be considered when representing the content of video, i.e., *movement* of actors and objects and *presence*, which is created out of the two parameters, *space* and *time*.

As suggested by the above, then, film engages the imagination of the viewer. This imagination is stimulated by two interacting structural systems within the film, these being the *narrative* (as realised through *montage*) and the *image* (as constructed via *Mise-en-scène*). *Montage* is the process of determining the narrative structure through the specific placement of shots, and is thus concerned with what might be called the *inter-shot* dimension of the film. *Mise-en-scène*, on the other hand, is concerned with the *intra-shot* dimension, with such factors as the direction of movement and physical attitude of characters, the point of view of the camera, the choice of lens, and so on. Since the relationship between montage and mise-en-scène is complex, it is useful to examine them separately. We begin with an analysis of film narrative, based on the discussion in Metz [17].

3.2. Narrativity

A narrative is the combination of two temporal schemata, one that tells the story and the other being the time over which the story is told. The established relation in a narrative is, therefore, a time-in-time relation, whereas any description creates a space-in-time relation and an image forms a space-within-space relation. A simple example should illustrate this. Imagine a sequence showing successive shots of the sea followed by a shot of a boat sailing across a stretch of water. The first motionless shot of the sea is simply an image of the sea (space-in-space), where the successive shots form a description of the area (space-in-time) and the crossing boat establishes the narrative (time-in-time). Thus, a narrative can be described as a system of temporal transformations.

A narrative arises from a description of a series of events, where each event can be either with or without a conclusion. The narrative realised in a film is always a closed sequence (the last image describes the definite end of the film). The ordering of events forms the narrative. From the spectator's point of view a film is pre-selected and pre-arranged material, which he or she attempts to understand. Figure 3 shows a diagrammatic representation of the relationship between film structure and story structure.

A necessary augmentation to the structure in figure 3 is an additional layer of description to deal with the plan structure of a story. This "meta-layer" formulates the story logic, at the single scene level, as a relationship between *motivation*, *theme realisation* and *resolution*. The motivation guides the spectator into the scene by providing hints as to the location of the action, the character, the character's emotional state, and so on. The theme realisation provides elements required to encourage the intended reaction of the spectators. The resolution supplies additional information for clarifying the intention of the scene, if this is necessary. For example, certain jokes require that the spectator actually sees the reaction of the character.

The motivation, theme realisation and resolution each reflect two distinct aims. Firstly, there is the *external reason* for telling the story. Depending on the intended overall mood of

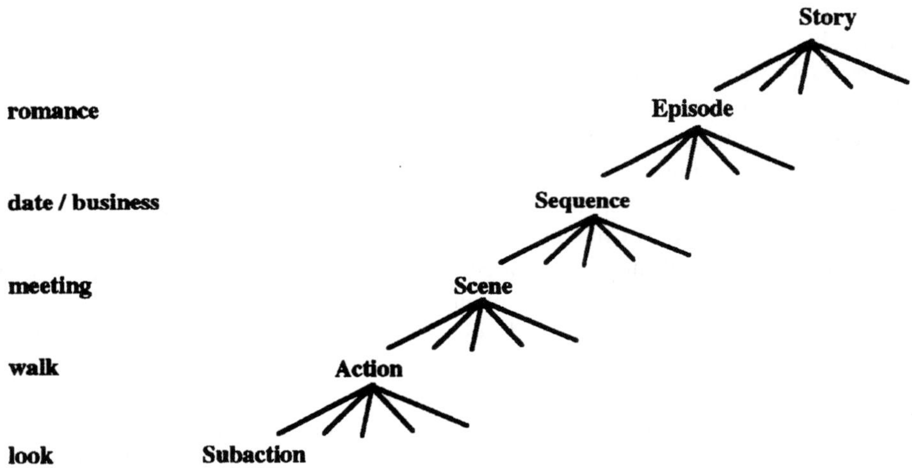

Figure 3. Story structure.

the scene (if it is to be humorous, for example), different thematic strategies for the creation of each of the three elements and the connection between them must be applied. Secondly, there is an *internal reason* within the story (e.g., the reason a character behaves in a particular way), which triggers the interest of the spectator. The internal and external reason must both be considered in creating a meaningful scene [36]. The effect of the three scene phases for the sharpening logic of a scene and with respect to the diminishing choice of appropriate visual material during the generation process is schematically represented in figure 4.

The same logical construction of motivation, theme realisation and resolution applies at the higher level of the interaction between scenes. However, the relationship between scenes

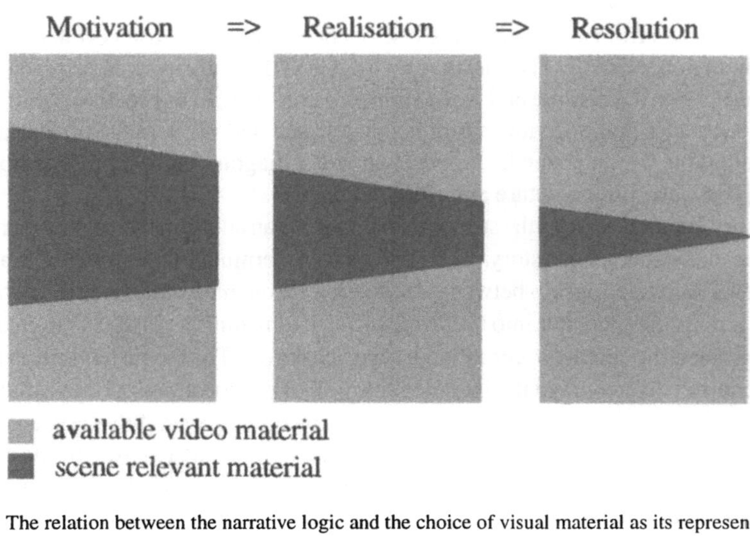

Figure 4. The relation between the narrative logic and the choice of visual material as its representation.

is more complex, since for scenes the semantic frame representing relationships between characters, situation oriented atmospheres, story rhythms, and so on, is much wider and richer than that pertaining between shots.

The underlying assumption of the above analyses is that a story is a psychological entity that refers to mental or conceptual objects such as *themes*, *goals*, *events* or *actions*. We believe that the logical structures underlying stories in films, books, plays or pantomime are essentially the same, though we acknowledge the significant differences between the perceptual aspects involved. These differences mean, for example, that it is inappropriate to directly apply the well established mechanisms for representing natural language understanding to film. The following sections present a brief survey of the underlying semantic, syntactic and semiotic factors that are specifically related to the perception of film.

3.3. Order and context

A landmark in the understanding of film perception was the Kuleshov experiments [14]. Kuleshov found that the juxtaposition of two unrelated images would force the viewer to find a connection between the two. In one experiment, described by Pudovkin [23], Kuleshov took a close-up shot of an actor, with a vacant expression, and intercut it with shots of a bowl of soup, a dead man and a lascivious woman to create three distinct sequences. Spectators to whom these three sequences were shown believed that the actor's facial expression showed hunger in the first sequence, sadness in the second and passion in the last. The experiments demonstrated two different aspects of our understanding of film, each influencing the other:

- The meaning of a shot depends on the context in which it is situated;
- A change in the order of shots within a scene changes the meaning of the shot as well as the meaning of the scene.

Experiments investigating the "Kuleshov effect" ascertained the variability of the meaning of a shot within different contexts (Goldberg, described in Isenhour [13], Foley, referenced by Isenhour [13]). Experiments concerning contextual details (e.g., direction of movement) were performed by Frith and Robson [10], who showed that a film sequence has a structure that can be described through selection rules and combination rules. An example is continuity of direction of movement, e.g., if a character leaves a shot to the right, we expect him to enter the next shot from the left.

Gregory [12] is responsible for detailed analysis of the importance of context and order in film editing. Gregory claims that not every combination of shots creates a meaning, but there are restricted conventions that can help create larger meaningful entities. His key elements for creating meaning by joining shots are *assertions* and *associative cues*.

An assertion is the relationship between two elements. There are many different types of such relationships. For example, the description of an attribute (such as *red* for a car) could be as important as a simple action (two men shaking hands). Consider a close-up of a woman who is looking down, followed by the image of a bowl in which a hand holding an electric mixer is preparing something. The assertion from this juxtaposition is that the woman shown in the first shot is preparing some food ([12], p. 39).

Gregory argues that a given shot, say A, can build divergent assertions with other shots by using various subsets of the information gathered from shot A. This is especially important since it means that the juxtaposition of shots can be analysed, as each shot has associated with it a variable collection of information, rather than a fixed visual description.

Associative cues result from the combination of various indicators that aid in the creation of meaning. Gregory introduces two main types of cues as being important in the making of assertions. The first type defines cues for the surrounding space. Most human activities, human roles or objects are associated with specific locations. The conceptualisation of space is, therefore, an elementary principle of the analysis and organisation within editing. The second type of cue is related to human actions, of which the above description of the shot of a woman cooking is an example.

If only a small number (or possibly no) cues are present in two juxtaposed images, both images may invite a combined interpretation by virtue of their ordering, but are nevertheless perceived by the viewer as isolated units. In such a case, the resulting combination is usually meaningless and might be irritating.

The main impact of Gregory's work is in showing that the juxtaposition of shots is subject to a situation plan, in which the action, emotional circumstances and timing of the potential scene are defined. It is this plan which makes editing possible [38].

There are yet two problems to be tackled. The first is how to represent associative cues and assertions and the second is how to map them onto the filmic material, so that the desired intellectual or emotional state of the viewer can be achieved. As we see in the next section, a discussion of various aspects of the semiology of film will enable a refinement of the requirements for our content based video representation.

3.4. Semantic fields and themes

A *sign*, in Saussure's terms, is in itself arbitrary and receives its expression by convention, as, in principle, every means of expression used in society is based on collective behaviour ([37], p. 117). A sign usually consists of two distinct components: the *signifier* (which caries the meaning) and the *signified* (which is the concept or thing signified). Since Saussure's approach to signs is linguistically motivated, Peirce and Jakobson suggest that a refinement is necessary in the case of cinematic signs. In their scheme, a cinematic sign can be of three types:

- **Icon.** A sign which represents its object mainly by similarity. There exist two sub-classes of icons: *images* and *diagrams*. In images simple qualities are alike (a portrait) whereas diagrams capture some aspects of the relationship between parts. In this paper we are concerned only with images.
- **Index.** A sign which represents its object by an inherent relationship. Examples: A man with a rolling gait can indicate drunkenness, a sundial or clock can indicate the time of day.
- **Symbol.** An arbitrary sign, where signifier and signified are not related and where the representation is based on convention.

With reference to the above, we now discuss *semantic fields*, which are one appropriate way of dealing with Gregory's cues, as discussed above. A semantic field is a set of relations between conceptual and linguistic units [4, 8]. The complexity of the conceptual structures that support the interpretation or creation of meaningful film sequences is described in Eco [8]. Eco argues that the analysis of cinematic signs is based on a socially determined reticular system of small semantic systems and rules for their combination. The organisational structure of a semantic field reflects various structures [4], such as

- *clusters:* terms within a semantic field that overlap semantically, e.g., *synonyms*
- *doublets:* semantic fields organised on the basis of polarities, e.g., *oppositions*
- *proportional series:* a series of oppositional doublets, e.g., *female-male*, *passive-active*, *womb-phallus*, etc.
- *hierarchies:* ordered semantic units based on relations of inclusion or *exclusion Pekinese/ dog/animal/living thing* [4]

A semantic field is therefore 'a conceptual structure which organises potential meanings in relation to others' ([4], p. 106).

Conceptual structures, as discussed above, are invoked in Spike Lee's movie "Do the right thing", which portrays 24 hours of a stiflingly hot day in Brooklyn (see picture 2). The concept of *hotness* is formed by showing "hot" colours (a *red* wall as background for a group of people sitting under a sunshade), *dancing* children under the *fountain of water* of a hydrant, or by the use of certain *light*. In Bergman's film "Shame", *money* is seen to be placed beside the head of the main *female* character (see picture 3), who is lying on a *bed*, which creates the concept *prostitution*.

An alternative way of dealing with cues is to use *themes*. A theme can be defined as the actual arrangement and presentation of narrative events according to specific principles. A theme can therefore be seen as a tactic, or schema, providing strategies to achieve a certain effect (e.g., humour) or adopting the position of a start point within a semantic field to provide a "meaning" for the visual presentation.

As our chosen exemplar theme, we consider *humour*. Many theories of humour exist and can usually be placed in one of three classes. The *cognitive-perceptual class* is associated with *incongruity* [30]. The central supposition of this theory is that humour is associated with

Picture 2. Taken from Spike Lee's Do the right thing (1989).

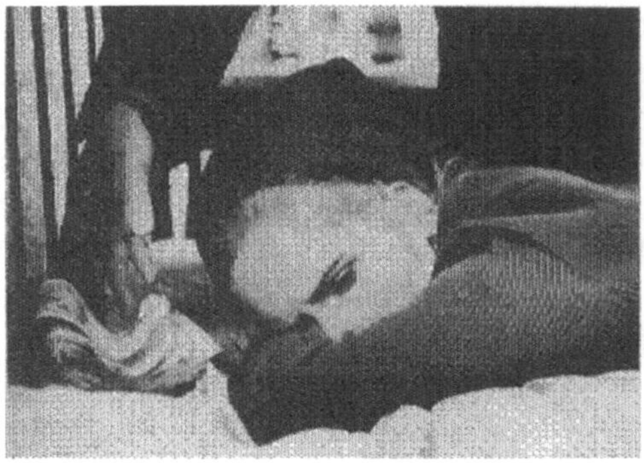

Picture 3. Liv Ullmann in Bergman's Shame (1968).

the unexpected outcome of a phrase or action, or with elements such as inappropriateness, paradox, or dissimilarity. The *social-behavioural class* considers humour to result from the infirmity or deformity of others, or where one party maligns, or is aggressive to, another [15]. Much ethnically motivated humour is of this form. The *psychoanalytical class* considers humour as a relief from constraints—such as to be logical, to think clearly, to talk sense—applying to human beings [9]. This line of research on humour deals with suppression or repression and is mostly concerned with tendentious humour, of which sexual humour is one example.

Each theory emphasises certain aspects of humour, but all rely on certain strategies, i.e., the modification of stereotypical actions, situations or behaviour involving elements such as *incongruity*, *stupidity*, *misfortune* and, if necessary, their *repetition*.

The combination of semantic fields and themes enables the creation of cues. However, there is still the problem of associating cues with the filmic material. This can be achieved by converting visual concepts, the most important of these being *movement* and *point of view*, into linguistic units which are then mapped onto the semantic fields.

3.5. Summary

From the above discussion, it can be concluded that film syntax determines film semantics, based on the syntagmatic connotation of successive shots. We clearly need to describe *shots* as objectively as possible, in order to facilitate their use in different sequences. A shot is defined as a single piece of film, however long or short, without cuts, exposed continuously. The content description must also be able to represent a still image (the single frame), which is the smallest unit within a shot, since the final frame of one shot, and the first frame of another, must be considered when joining two shots together.

It should be emphasised that narrative elements should not be part of the content description of a shot. An event is not necessarily *objectively visible*, but rather based on inferences encouraged by the ordering of shots and the viewer's expectations and background knowledge. Therefore, the representation of images should be as objective as possible, in order to facilitate the reuse of such images in various narratives. It is thus important that the representation of a narrative is maintained in such a way that various film realisations of such a narrative can be constructed [19].

4. A proposed architecture for theme oriented video creation

In this section we present an architecture for the automated creation of video scenes. Figure 5 shows a overview of this architecture. The architecture embodies aspects of the editing model, the theories of humour, and the conceptual framework for the creation of thematic scenes, discussed above. The architecture is realised in the current version of our experimental system AUTEUR, implemented in Sicstus Prolog on a SUN Sparc workstation. The section concludes with the schematic description of a humorous scene that was actually generated by AUTEUR.

4.1. Video database

The video database is an arbitrary collection of digitised video material. Our work is not concerned with the different possible formats for digital video, though our current implementation uses the MPEG format. For experimental purposes, the video database is currently restricted to approximately 40 shots, each between 1 and 15 seconds in length, and filmed by the first author.

4.2. Video representation

Our video representation formalism is designed so that objectivity of shot description can be maintained. This supports the reuse of shots, as was discussed earlier.

The description of each shot is hierarchical, descending from general features to specific details. Each shot description contains a header, descriptions of cinematographic devices

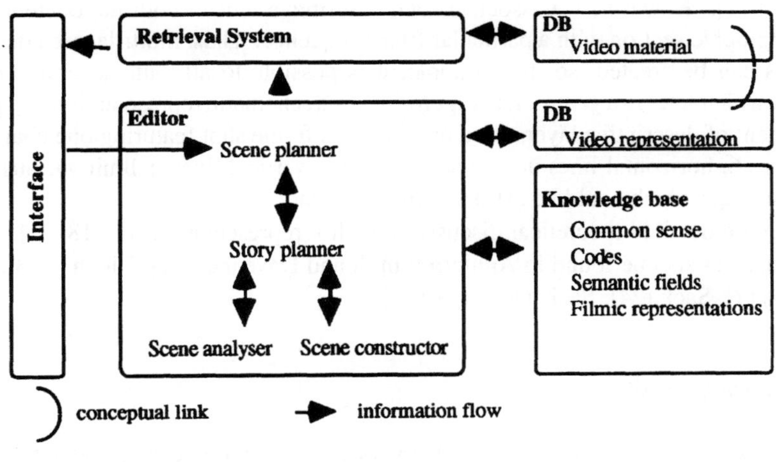

Figure 5. Architecture of AUTEUR.

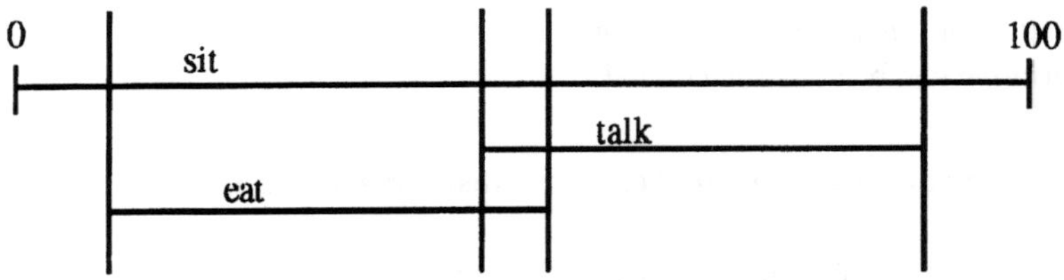

Figure 6. Actions annotated in layers in a 100 frame shot.

and information about the *shot content*. As our representation is language oriented, we have to ensure that any overly directive choice of labelling does not occur. This is achieved by the use of generic terms. For example, instead of instantiating the *action* of an *actor* as *gorge*, which implies *greed*, only the most general term *eat* is allowed. By considering the *speed* of the action and the wider context, the system might then conclude the manifestation of *greed*, or it may reject this interpretation. In this way, then, the objective representation of a shot supports, but does not uniquely determine, the interpretation.

To facilitate the use of filmic codes to influence scene generation, the description of cinematic devices includes information regarding the length of a shot, its start and end frame and the shot type, as well as information about the state of the lens and the camera, the colour of the shot (which can either be black and white, or, if colour, the dominant impression), and the contrast of the shot, e.g., high, low, etc.

The content part of the shot representation is subdivided into two nested structures, the *foreground* and *background*, each containing denotative information about the image, i.e., mise-en-scène (time, location), the appearance of a character (age, race, etc.), the actions of a character (action, speed of the action, direction of movement, etc.), the appearance of objects and the events in which those objects are involved, and various relationships between different shot elements (e.g., character A is left of object B, object B is behind object C, etc.).

We use a stratified representation of scenes, as first introduced by Aguierre Smith and Davenport [1]. However, we associate each descriptive unit in both the content and the cinematographic section with a particular frame sequence. Thus, multi-layered descriptive structures can be created, so, for example, it is possible to attribute several concurrent actions to a character in a given shot. Figure 6 gives a schematic representation of a possible arrangement of descriptive layers for a one-hundred frame shot featuring one character.

In figure 6, horizontal lines denote actions, while vertical lines delimit various content based film clips which could be extracted from this shot.

For a more detailed theoretical discussion of shot representation see [18–21]. Related approaches can also be found in Aguierre Smith and Davenport [1], Bloch [2, 3], Carroll [6], Davis [7], Sack [24], Sack and Davis [25].

4.3. *Knowledge base*

The *knowledge base* contains conceptual structures representing events and actions, along with representations of visual features underpinned by a network of semantic fields.

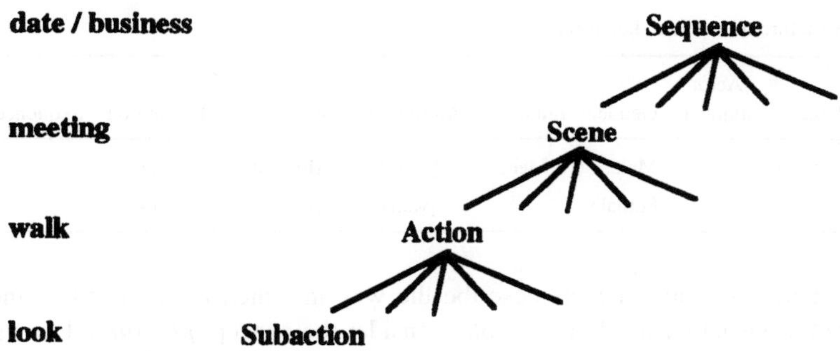

Figure 7. Relevant story structure for AUTEUR.

As stated earlier, we currently consider only single scenes. We therefore define only those structures from figure 3 (overall story structure) that are subordinate to scenes, as is illustrated in figure 7.

Our representation of actions is influenced by that used in Lehnert et al. [16], Schank [28], Schank and Abelson [29]. Each action is part of a network structure that supports the following links:

- *subaction links*, that point to actions performed concurrently to, and that form a conceptual unity with, a main action, such as *walk* and *look*. These links are given tags from an arbitrary qualitative modal scale, e.g., necessary, non-essential, etc.
- *opposition links*, that indicate antonymous actions
- *synonym links*
- *ambiguity links*, that indicate actions serving as subactions for other actions, e.g., for both of the actions "cry" and "laugh" a subaction might be "shake"
- *association links*, pointing to actions that can be associated with the current action, e.g., "sit" and "listen"
- *intention links*, linking actions that relate to the goal of an action.

Each action is further described as a concept containing descriptions of such features as the objects the action involves, the body parts of the actor involved in the action, spatial relationships between the objects and body parts, the locations of the action, relationships between the objects and the location, the state of an actor after the action is performed, and possible reactions.

The structure of a scene is represented by an event, which is described by its name, the number of actors or objects involved and their gender, the intentional action, the main actions of the actors involved, and a link to the next higher element within the story structure. The part of the main actions is divided into the three event stages, *motivation*, *realisation* and *resolution*, each of them containing a sequence of actions for each actor. Table 1 shows a simplified event representation for a "meeting".

Sequences are described by scripts that feature descriptions of the type of characters involved, their appearance, their mood and a collection of events for the motivation, realisation and resolution stages.

Table 1. Structure of an event, i.e., *meeting*.

Name	Actor number	Gender	Intention	Motivation	Realisation	Resolution	Sequence
Meeting	2	Male, Female	Meet	[walk] [wait]	[look at] [look at]	[walk] [walk]	Date

Visual representation concepts describe the way in which an intended theme can be represented in visual terms. For example, consider the concept *pleasure*. Pleasure might be expressed by a smile, or through actions being performed at medium speed, giving the impression that the character is relaxed. The combination of both offers a stronger visual impression than the appearance of only one of the alternatives. One definition of a smile is that it can be identified through the appearance of lips, which should curve up. The visual concept is, therefore, the link between a story element, e.g., the intention of an actor, and the representation of the shot, where the link determines the instantiation of the important elements from the shot representation. Such visual representation concepts are used in each step of the scene creation process.

Finally, the system contains hierarchically organised conceptual knowledge about objects, locations, directions and moods.

4.4. Scene planner

The task of the scene planner (see figure 5) is to organise the strategies for realising the required theme. An important factor is the *motive* for showing the scene. The motive may vary, i.e., we might wish the viewer to be *convinced*, *impressed*, *informed* or *emotionally attached*. However, the chosen *external point* [35, 36] will influence the scene structure. In this paper, as discussed earlier, we focus on the theme of humour.

The scene planner is involved in the creation process from the outset, by providing the analysis of the startshot. This analysis, based on the shot description in the video representation, provides information about the number of actors, groups of actors, objects and groups of objects. Each of these units is related to particular information about their actions, i.e., sequences of actions, actions performed concurrently (i.e., performed during the same sequence of frames), and single actions. The mood of actors and groups of actors is analysed using heuristics referring to visual expressions or the speed of an action. The result is a mood description, such as ‘pleasure’, combined with a numeric value that represents the system’s certainty that the mood is suggested by the chosen material. Finally, the analysis contains information about the location (e.g., indoors/outdoors, relevant objects, etc.).

The earlier discussion identified three key strategies for the generation of visual humour, i.e., *incongruity*, *stupidity* and *misfortune*. Guided by these three strategies, the scene planner plans the various steps necessary for the generation process. Typical heuristics used to guide the scene planner’s decisions are:

- a joke that contradicts the viewer’s expectations is preferable to a straightforwardly presented one,

- actions form a preferable basis for a joke than actors, then objects and finally location,
- a sequence of actions is more preferable than parallel or single actions since no motivation needs to be created in the former case,
- parallel actions provide more possibilities for jokes than single actions,
- when only a single action is available, the *misfortune* strategy should be used before that for *stupidity* and finally *incongruity*,
- if parts of an actor, e.g., the face, are not visible, adopt the "incongruity" strategy.

For each of the three generation phases, i.e., motivation, realisation and resolution, the scene planner provides the story planner with a plan description which contains details of the strategy to be used. For the last two phases, however, the scene planner requires feedback from the story planner that describes the actual status of the ongoing story, which is provided by an interpretation package holding information about the meaning of the story, the motivated event, mood, action, actors involved, etc. Depending on this information the scene planner might change direction within the strategy. For example, a new character may have been introduced due to motivational requirements, and must now be included in the storyline. It is even possible for the scene planner to select a completely different strategy. It might be the case, for example, that the strategy *misfortune* could produce a storyline but there is not enough visual material to support the story. A way out of this dilemma is to apply an alternative strategy, for example *stupidity*, to the already retrieved material.

The scene planner is also responsible for decisions as to how particular events within an episode should be realised, i.e., whether the events should be shown in parallel or series. For example, if there is only one character it is sufficient to portray the different humorous scenes sequentially, whereas with two characters it might be more appropriate to portray their different actions alternately, bringing the two characters together only in the final scene.

Finally, the scene planner evaluates the end result. For each of the different generation phases it establishes the extent to which the required content and stylistic units can be fulfilled. Since AUTEUR stores details of jokes it has previously created, it avoids re-creating the same joke twice.

4.5. Story planner

While the scene planner is concerned with the external point, or theme, of the scene, the *story planner* is concerned with its *internal* point [35, 36]. The story planner specifies the content of the scene, and is therefore responsible for the detailed application of a particular strategy. The humour strategies embodied in the story planner can be described as follows:

Misfortune. Try to foil the character so that unexpected results occur which downgrade his or her mood in the situation, but without causing major or fatal damage. A typical example is found in slapstick situations, such as being hit by a cake.

Incongruity. Try to generate an unexpected outcome for an action, by introducing elements such as *inappropriateness*, *paradox*, *dissimilarity* or *ambiguity*. An example should demonstrate this (taken from the Chaplin film *The Immigrants*). The scene is set on a rolling boat. Chaplin is leaning over the rail and his legs are fluttering in the air. We automatically assume he is suffering from a heavy attack of seasickness. However, when he turns around we see that he was simply fishing.

Stupidity. Try to generate a scene where a sequence of events is performed such that the end result makes no sense and the character is therefore assumed to be stupid. The following example is taken from Mike Leigh's film *Naked*: A man pastes a poster on a wall (advertising a concert). He leaves the place in his van. He arrives at another place where the poster is already pasted on a wall. He pastes a stripe over it, stating "cancelled".

Depending on the strategy and its specification provided by the scene planner, the story planner uses the conceptual structures from the knowledge base referring to actions, moods, persons, events and locations to attempt to construct a coherent scene.

A further important task of the story planner is to determine the point of view from which the story is seen to be taking place. For example, the story planner must decide whether it is appropriate to tell the story from a particular character's perspective. The two points of view implemented in AUTEUR at this time are the third person narrative style and the reaction shot. These are sufficient to create the intended kind of humorous scenes.

The story planner consists of three independent planners, one for each creation phase. The motivation, realisation and resolution planner are essentially specialists for the content generation of the scene. They use the plan list and interpretation package as primary resources, and each collaborate with the scene analyser and the scene creator to establish the visual presentation of their respective part of the scene.

4.6. *Scene analyser*

The *scene analyser* supervises the retrieval of the required video material. The content based query is provided by one of the motivation, realisation or resolution planners, depending on the current generation phase. The aim of the scene analyser is to collect the most appropriate video material in terms of content and style. The mechanisms used are a representation of the permissible relations between shots, as described in Table 2, and a collection of editing codes.

In AUTEUR, shots can be juxtaposed in essentially three ways: putting one shot either immediately before, immediately after, or inserting it within, another. Based on a classification of shot types developed by Dziga Vertov (described in Petric [22]), which describes the seven shot types used in Table 2, AUTEUR can determine the most suitable type of shot to be retrieved. For example, suppose that the object of a given long shot needs to be highlighted for motivational requirements. The scene analyser contains rules to determine a favourable shot for a given intention, e.g., an insert corresponds with *highlighting*. The most appropriate shot kind for an insert is a close-up. Nevertheless, as shown in Table 2, a long shot can be joined with another long shot or with closely related shot types (those marked X in Table 2). Since the aim of AUTEUR is to construct a clearly perceptible scene, the system attempts to fulfil the close-up approach by finding a suitable bridging shot, so that a long shot and a close-up can be joined.

The order of shot types is as specified in Table 2, in that the minimal shot type is an extreme close-up and the maximal shot type is an extreme long shot. Shot types are

Table 2. Joining relations between shots.

	Shot B						
Shot A	(1)	(2)	(3)	(4)	(5)	(6)	(7)
(1) Extreme close-up	X	X					
(2) Close-up	X	X	X				
(3) Medium close-up		X	X	X			
(4) Medium			X	X	X		
(5) Medium long				X	X	X	
(6) Long					X	X	X
(7) Extreme long						X	X

therefore represented as a one dimensional vector. AUTEUR uses the distance between two shot types in this vector to determine if a bridging shot is necessary when joining the two shots. This involves gathering, in order, every shot type in the vector between the first shot type and the second shot type. The resulting list is a specification of the "bridge".

Returning to our example, the scene analyser is attempting to determine an appropriate bridging sequence for the join of a long shot with a close up. Using the bridging technique specified above, the recommended shot type ordering would be:

first part of long shot, medium shot, close-up, second part of long shot.

If the recommended shot types are unavailable, back up rules are used, such as "if the highlight is an insert and there is material which is of the kind *close-up* insert it".

The shot type, while important, is but one criterion affecting the retrieval process. A second important requirement is *continuity*, which can only be determined by examining the content descriptions of the shots to be joined, as is now discussed.

The scene analyser assesses the continuity between two shots by comparing the mise-en-scène and content descriptions of the two shots. The order in which the shots are to be joined dictates how this comparison is carried out. For example, when following a long shot by a medium shot it is advisable that all the elements within the medium shot are represented in the long shot. This is not the case if a medium shot is followed by a long shot.

The scene analyser uses editing rules to direct the ordering of shots such as:

- for highlighting use a zoom-in,
- use soft focus to portray romantic moods,
- use low-angle shots to emphasise the dominance of a character,

and so on.

Each such editing rule has an associated applicability value, which is added to the evaluation value of a shot if the particular editing rule is applicable. The shot with the highest evaluation value is ultimately chosen. The outcome of the creation process is an ordered list of shots, and type specifications (if a shot is an 'insert', a 'long shot', and so on), which will eventually form the scene.

If the scene analyser is unable to retrieve visual material, as requested by the story planner, spatial and general knowledge structures from the knowledge base are used to decompose the query into sub-queries. At this stage, the algorithms we use to perform this kind of *query restructuring* are rudimentary. Butler [5], describes a more sophisticated approach to the problem of decomposing non-filmically expressed queries into film editing specifications.

In cases where no material can be found to realise a particular narrative, the scene analyser notifies the story planner, which alters the storyline until a scene is successfully created.

4.7. Scene constructor

The *scene constructor* receives the annotated scene list from the scene analyser, and actually performs the detailed joining of the specified shots.

The scene constructor contains editing knowledge on a *cutting* level. This can mean that a shot is truncated, if it is too long for the purpose required (e.g., two seconds exposure to a close up is often sufficient for the viewer to appreciate what is being shown). Cuts may also be motivated if only part of a particular shot is required. This can be of particular importance in maintaining continuity, for example, in the case of inserts that break the flow of action, but where the actual screening time of the insert must be taken into consideration.

The output from the scene constructor is an ordered list of the shot identifiers, along with frame numbers for each shot. This list specifies the scene that is to be displayed.

4.8. Retrieval system and interface

The *retrieval system* adapts the final stream of shot ids and frame numbers (produced by the scene constructor) into a file specifying the actual presentation of the scene. The file lists the appropriate MPEG files along with associated start and end frames, which can be shown in a small "projection" window on the workstation. The presentation environment is written in X and uses SUN Video Technology/XI Library.

5. The creation of a visual joke

We now consider an example to show how the different elements of our architecture combine to produce a humorous sequence of film. For clarity, the example has been simplified. Note that actual shots of film are involved in the actual scene created, but that we depict the shots below by using only a single image from each shot.

Imagine a start sequence as given in shot 1. The system begins with an analysis of the representation of the given shot, in terms of *number of characters*, *objects* or *groups*, related *actions*, *moods* and *location*. The construction of the mood is based on visual expressions and actions (type, speed, order) related to an actor. The result is a list of possible moods, such as pleasure, hurry, etc., each tagged with a certainty value that must be higher than 0.35 for a mood to be considered. The following is an example of the type of analysis which

Shot 1

may be extracted by the scene planner:

Shotkind = long
Actors = 1, ID = Paul
Actions: sequence: no, parallel: no, single action: walk
Mood: pleasure + 0.5, hurry + 0.5
Objects: 2, ID = path, meadow
Group-Object: 1, ID = trees.

The scene planner uses this information to decide on the most suitable humour strategy to be applied. Suppose the resulting plan is that the joke to be produced should be single-person single-action oriented. Since the joke is to be based on a single action, AUTEUR will suggest the misfortune strategy. This strategy requires a mood deterioration which automatically provokes a check on the mood as well as the shot kind. Since the shot is a long shot, and the mood is indeterminate in both cases, the scene planner now requires a motivation for both the mood and the event.

In the light of the chosen strategy, the story planner attempts to create a motivation for a mood and an event. The aim is to create a visual representation that makes it clear that the person is either in a good mood or is in a real hurry. Furthermore, the mood should correspond with the event to be created.

AUTEUR first attempts to establish a suitable mood. The knowledge base contains a number of mood concepts, along with related actions. For example, *pleasure* might be associated with smiling, whistling, the picking of flowers, and so on. Comparing the actual shot representation with the proposed mood related actions, AUTEUR infers that a person can walk and smile at the same time. Since the mood certainty value of a smile, with respect to *pleasure*, is high, the story planner has identified a suitable event. A query is sent to the scene analyser to retrieve an appropriate visual representation. The query specifies the underlying intention for the material (i.e., highlighting a mood), the required character, and the action (i.e., smile).

Suppose that the scene planner finds shots related to the required mood (*pleasure*), for the given character, as shown in shots 2, 3 and 4. From these, the system chooses shot 3, as its content description indicates that it most obviously presents the mood, is consistent with the direction of action, and represents a zoom-in.

Establishing the mood enables the story planner to specify further events by constructing an appropriate goal for the character. One such goal might be to meet another person. Thus,

Shot 2

Shot 3

Shot 4

the story planner attempts to construct a meeting using event and scene structures. Possible event structures might be a male meeting a female for a date, and so on. Assume that the system tries to create the event *meeting*. For the *motivation* phase, the story planner uses parts of the event structure which are necessary for establishing that a meeting is expected to take place, such as one person waiting and the other walking, or perhaps both characters walking. Since, in our example, the action of one character is already specified, AUTEUR must find an corresponding action for the other character. This is the basis for the query sent to the scene analyser, which suggests shot 5 as appropriate.

The scene constructor places the shots in the required order, i.e., 5, 1, 3, 1 and the interpretation of the motivation sequence is transferred to the scene planner for further plan specification. The scene analyser introduces a new character and selects the plan for person-person related joke.

Since one character's state is passive ("waiting"), and the potential main character is active ("walking"), the inference drawn is that the joke is to be based on the action. Hence, the full joke is to be a person-person single action related joke. The strategy, *misfortune*, does not need to be changed. The next step is the realisation of the *theme*, and therefore the scene planner must consider the constraints that must be applied to produce the humour. For a single action there are two constraints: the mishap should be simple, and unexpected by the main character.

One of the strategies for creating a misfortune is to violate a character's goal. Since the intention is derived from the action, the story planner attempts to select an event that will foil the main action. Analysing the oppositional links of "walk", optional actions appear,

Shot 5

such as such as *fall*, *slip*, *stumble*, or *collide with.* In decreasing order of the values of the oppositional links for *walk*, the story planner attempts to instantiate the oppositional concept. Take *slip* as an example. The conceptual description of *slip* contains details of objects a character might slip on, body parts involved, spatial relationships between the objects and body parts, locations slipping can occur, relationships between the objects and the location, the state of a character after the event occurs, and states that might result from the occurrence of the event.

The conceptual structure of slip is the source for a number of queries to the scene analyser, considered in descending order of suitability, such as:

- find a shot where the actor *slips*, where the object the character slips on is found in the startshot,
- find a shot where a body part *slips* on an object, where the object is found in the startshot,
- find a shot where the actor performs an action that is related to *slip*, and a shot showing an object that is also related to *slip*,
- find a shot where the actor performs a *slip* related action.

Suppose that the first query above is not satisfied, but that the second is successful. The story planner then requests a shot of the object the character is to slip on, as the spectator will then anticipate the mishap and this is predicted to increase the potential success of the joke.

The scene analyser then analyses the content and style of the potential material, following which the scene constructor specifies the actual detailed joining of the material. The final outcome is a two-shot scene as suggested by the stills in picture 4.

An additional outcome of the realisation phase is an extended information package, summarising the content and filmic aspects of the current joined material. This information is used by the scene planner to validate the currently used strategy.

A *resolution* may be necessary. Following the *misfortune*, a resolution is required to portray the mood change. Since such information cannot be found in the material constructed so far, the request for a resolution phase becomes part of the plan structure.

Using the conceptual structure for *slip*, the story planner constructs requests for video material that portrays an appropriate reaction by the character, to *slipping*. The reactions are composed by considering possible resulting states and, if pertinent, the relevant object.

Picture 4. Scene part generated out of two shots.

Shot 6

For the case of *slip* and *banana skin*, one possibility is to request a shot of the character lying on the ground, or a shot of the character looking angrily down at either the *banana skin* or something not represented in the shot, or a shot of the character simply looking angry, and so on. The selection of the best shot (if several are found) is based on the value of the link between the action and the related concepts to the action from the descriptions of the retrieved shots.

The shot history, i.e., the joins used so far, is considered by the scene planner in order to support the creation of a coherent presentation, by ensuring that constancy of filmic style is maintained throughout the scene (examples being the consistent use of close-ups for highlighting, or cutting without bridging). This is particularly important in the generation of *repetition*. Shot 6 shows a frame from a shot that realises these aims with respect to the existing chosen material.

The scene planner next seeks options for developing further jokes from the existing story line. If this cannot be done, the scene planner attempts to provide the specification of an appropriate conclusion to the scene. Typical strategies activated to achieve these aims are:

- seek additional interfering actions,
- repeatedly apply the *misfortune* strategy, e.g., in our *meeting* example, the main character may continue to attempt to reach the meeting after slipping on the banana skin, and may be subjected to further mishaps, such as missing a bus, failing to hail a taxi, and so on,
- if the joke is person-person related, arrange the different segments so that the characters fulfil their goals.

Let us assume, for simplicity, that visual material for all three of the above strategies is unavailable. The scene planner then examines the specification of the constructed scene and detects that there is superfluous material, i.e., the additionally introduced character. This will initiate a re-editing plan, which is performed by the scene constructor. The final version of the banana skin joke, which is roughly 20 seconds long, is suggested by the stills in picture 5.

Finally, the scene planner evaluates the visual joke on the basis of information gathered in the interpretation package. In the example here, each of the generation phases produces the required content, though with varying degree of success. The value of the stylistic units

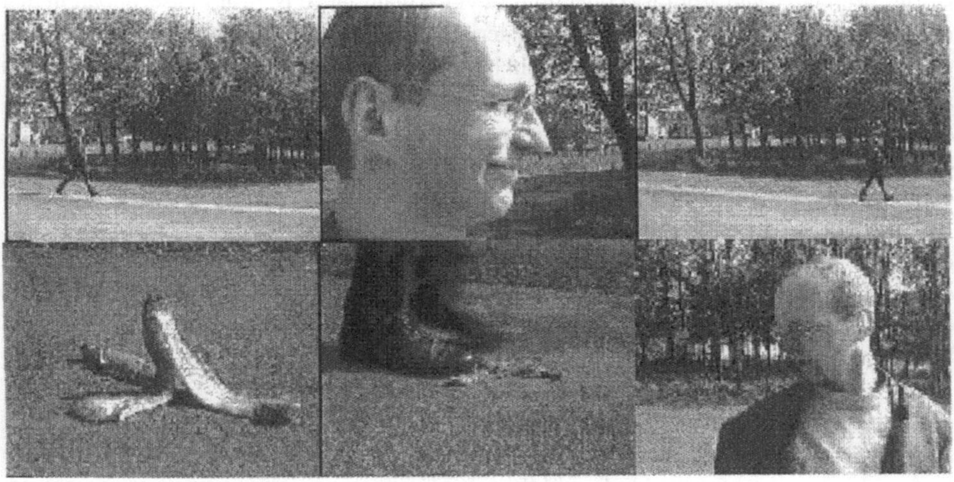

Picture 5. The final humorous scene.

is high enough for a good ranking. The overall verdict is therefore "good", even though the originality is assessed as not above average.

Further details of the content and duration of the shots used in the final scene are given in an appendix.

6. Conclusion

In order to develop our model of editing, the first author performed a "knowledge elicitation" exercise involving studying and interviewing editors at work in their own environment, i.e., the cutting rooms of the WDR[1]. In common with those involved in the enterprise of knowledge elicitation in other domains, we found that the expertise of the editors could not be codified in the form of simple rules. The complexity involved in the video editing process is obscured by the fact that those involved appear to manage it effortlessly, even though many different influences, and knowledge at varying levels and detail, are involved. Some of the complexity of the task is reflected in the different dimensions of our AUTEUR architecture.

We are aware that the approach described in this article is only a small step towards the intelligent editing of video. Nevertheless, we believe that the work undertaken will provide input into research on the automated generation of video scenes and also on the interpretation and analysis of video. However, there are problems associated with our approach that remain to be addressed.

AUTEUR is a research platform, and as such achieves limited success in using relatively neutral material to suggest a given theme. The current version of AUTEUR produces only a restricted range of humorous scenes, predominantly of the so-called *slapstick* style, e.g., "slipping on the banana-peel". However, AUTEUR does do this in ways that take account of knowledge of what constitutes filmic acceptability. At this moment in time, we make no claim as to the general applicability of the techniques embodied in AUTEUR for creating stories from large and arbitrary collections of video material. It is, in any case, apparent that the notion of arbitrary re-use of video material is illusory, since in general, the computational effort involved in comparing content based descriptions to establish continuity would result in an unacceptable degradation of system performance. However, if the mechanisms described in this article are used for *domain dependent applications*, a suitable selection of material would reduce this complexity. For example, we may ensure that our database contains only shots in which:

- a small set of characters are found in similar locations,
- the locations are simple,
- the actions are available from different angles, point of views, etc.

Our earlier discussion of the nature of film editing demonstrates that we are also aware of the cultural and subjective influences on the editing process. We appreciate the problems of attempting to represent such influences. In a small way, the influences of subjectivity can be found in our use of valued links and the ways in which our semantic nets are organised.

At present, we are engaged in research into richer strategies for visual humour, and the generation of larger structural story entities such as *sequences*. The AUTEUR system and its theoretical foundation are best regarded as a platform that demonstrates the possibility of automated thematic film editing in restricted, yet complex, domains.

Appendix: Details of shots used in the "banana skin" joke

Shot 1: duration: 5.5 sec
content: Frank goes from the left to the right side of the screen
cuts: In the final joke this makes shots 1 and 3. The smile is an insert.

Shot 2: duration: 2.5 sec
content: Frank's head in close up
cut: entire shot used

Shot 3: duration: 11 sec
content: banana skin lying on a path
cut: first 2.5 seconds only used

Shot 4: duration: 3.3 sec
content: shows a shoe slipping on a banana peel
cut: entire shot used

Shot 5: duration: 3.5 sec
content: shows Frank turning around, and looking down angrily
cut: entire shot used

Total length of scene: 18.8 sec.

Acknowledgments

This project is supported by Lancaster University. We also thank the WDR (Westdeutscher Rundfunk—Köln) and the BR (Bayrischer Rundfunk—München) for supporting this work by offering access to their practical sessions.

Special thanks to Sean Butler for the video presentation software.

Note

1. WDR (Westdeutscher Rundfunk—Köln) is the biggest television broadcast station in Germany.

References

1. T.G. Aguierre Smith and G. Davenport, "The stratification system. A design environment for random access video," in ACM Workshop on Networking and Operating System Support for Digital Audio and Video, San Diego: California, 1992.
2. G.R. Bloch, "Elements d'une Machine de Montage Pour l'Audio-Visuel," Ph.D., Ecole Nationale Supérieure Des Télécommunications, 1986.
3. G.R. Bloch, "From concepts to film sequences," in RIAO 88, MIT Cambridge: MA, pp. 760–767, 1988.
4. D. Bordwell, Making Meaning—Inference and Rhetoric in the Interpretation of Cinema, Harvard University Press: Cambridge, Massachusetts, 1989.
5. S. Butler, "Automatic intelligent video editing, an implementation and some cinema theoretic consequences," (Technical report), Lancaster University, 1995.
6. J.M. Carroll, Toward a Structural Psychology of Cinema, Mouton Publishers: The Hague, 1980.
7. M. Davis, "Media streams: Representing Video for Retrieval and Repurposing," Ph.D., MIT, 1995.
8. U. Eco, Einführung in Die Semiotik, Wilhelm Fink Verlag: München, 1985.
9. S. Freud, Jokes and their Relation to the Unconscious, Routledge & Kegan Paul Ltd: London, 1960.
10. U. Frith and J.E. Robson, "Perceiving the language of film," Perception, Vol. 4, pp. 97–103, 1975.
11. A.S. Gordon and E.A. Domeshek, "Conceptual indexing for video retrieval," in IJCAI 95-Workshop on Intelligent Multimedia Information Retrieval, Montréal, Canada, 19th of Aug. 1995.
12. J.R. Gregory, "Some Psychological Aspects of Motion Picture Montage," Ph.D. Thesis, University of Illinois, 1961.
13. J.P. Isenhour, "The effects of context and order in film editing," AV Communication Review, Vol. 23, No. 1, pp. 69–80, 1975.
14. L. Kuleshov, Kuleshov on Film—Writing of Lev Kuleshov, University of California Press: Berkeley, 1974.
15. L. La Fave, J. Haddad, and W.A. Maesen, "Superiority, enhanced self-esteem, and perceived incongruity humour theory," in Humor and Laughter: Theory, Research and Applications, T. Chapman and H. Foot (Eds.), John Wiley & Sons: New York, pp. 63–91, 1976.
16. W.G. Lehnert, M.G. Dyer, P.N. Johnson, C.J. Yang, and S. Harley, "BORIS—An experiment in in-depth understanding of narratives," Artificial Intelligence, Vol. 20, pp. 15–62, 1983.
17. C. Metz, Film Language: A Semiotic of the Cinema, Oxford University Press: New York, 1974.
18. F. Nack and A. Parkes, "The role of video semantics in automated video editing," (Technical report—unpublished), Lancaster University, 1994.
19. A.P. Parkes, "An Artificial Intelligence Approach to the Conceptual Description of Videodisc Images," Ph.D. Thesis, Lancaster University, 1989a.
20. A.P. Parkes, "The prototype CLORIS system: Describing, retrieving and discussing videodisc stills and sequences," Information Processing and Management, Vol. 25, No. 2, pp. 171–186, 1989b.
21. A.P. Parkes, "Settings and the settings structure: The description and automated propagation of networks for perusing videodisk image atates," in SIGIR'89, N.J. Belkin and C.J. van Rijsbergen (Eds.), Cambridge, MA, pp. 229–238, 1989c.
22. V. Petric, Constructivism in Film, Cambridge University Press: Cambridge, 1987.

23. V.I. Pudovkin, Film Technique and Film Acting, Vision Press Limited: London, 1968.
24. W. Sack, "Coding news and popular culture," in The International Joint Conference on Artificial Intelligence (IJCA93) Workshop on Models of Teaching and Models of Learning, Chambery, Savoie, France, 1993.
25. W. Sack and M. Davis, "IDIC: Assembling video sequences from story plans and content annotations," in IEEE International Conference on Multimedia Computing and Systems, Boston, Ma, May 14–19, 1994.
26. W. Sack and A. Don, Splicer: An Intelligent Video Editor (Unpublished Working Paper), MIT, 1993.
27. G. Salomon and A.A. Cohen, "Television formats, mastery of mental skills, and the acquisition of knowledge," Journal of Educational Psychology, Vol. 69, pp. 612–619, 1977.
28. R. Schank, Dynamic Memory, Cambridge University Press: New York, 1982.
29. R. Schank and R. Abelson, Scripts, Plans, Goals and Understanding, Hillsdale, Lawrence Erlbaum Associates: New Jersey, 1977.
30. T.R. Shultz, "A cognitive-developmental analysis of humor," in Humor and Laughter: Theory, Research and Applications, T. Chapman and H. Foot (Eds.), John Wiley and Sons: New York, pp. 11–36, 1976.
31. D. Swanberg, C.F. Shu, and R. Jain, "Architecture of a multimedia information system for content based retrieval," in Third International Workshop On Network And Operating System Support For Digital Audio And Video, San Diego: California, pp. 345–350, 1992.
32. Y. Tonomura, A. Akutsu, Y. Taniguchi, and G. Suzuki, "Structured video computing," IEEE MultiMedia, Vol. 1, No. 3, pp. 34–43, 1994.
33. A. Tudor, Image and Influence, George Allen & Unwin Ltd.: London, 1974.
34. H. Ueda, T. Miyatake, S. Sumino, and A. Nagasaka, "Automatic structure visualization for video editing," in ACM & IFIP INTERCHI'93, pp. 137–141, 1993.
35. R. Wilensky, "Points: A theory of the structure of stories in memory," in Strategies for Natural Language Processing, W.G. Lehnert and M.H. Ringle (Eds.), Hillsdale, Lawrence Erlbaum Associates: New Jersey, pp. 345–376, 1983a.
36. R. Wilensky, "Story grammars versus story points," The Behavioral and Brain Sciences, Vol. 6, No. 4, pp. 579–623, 1983b.
37. P. Wollen, Signs and Meaning in the Cinema, Thames & Hudson: London, 1970.
38. H.J. Wulff, "Der plan macht's," in Handbuch der Filmmontage—Praxis und Prinzipien des Filmschnitts, München: TR-Verlagsunion, H. Beller (Ed.), pp. 178–189, 1993.

Frank Nack received his B.Sc. in Computer Science from Fachhochschule Darmstadt in Germany (1989). After working for the Siemens AG telecommunication group in Munich, he earned his M.Sc. in Applied AI from Aberdeen University, Scotland (1991). After working for Swedish Telecom in Sweden, he joined the Applied AI group of the Computing Department at Lancaster University (1993), where he is currently finishing his Ph.D. thesis. His main areas of interest are AI and film semiology, video representation and automated visual storytelling.

Alan Parkes is a Lecturer in Computer Science in the Computing Department at Lancaster University. He graduated with first class honours in Computer Science from the University of Wolverhampton, in 1981. Following this, he took his Ph.D. in "An Artificial Intelligence Approach to the Conceptual Representation of Video Images", at Lancaster. Having been awarded his Ph.D., he spent 1998–90 as a postdoctoral research fellow, researching "User-Oriented Content-Based Multimedia Explanations". Since then he has led a group of researchers at Lancaster that comprises members from the Applied AI and Distributed Multimedia Research Groups, this research being sponsored by the Engineering and Physical Sciences Research Council, and several companies. The main thrust of his research is conceptual representation of video to support automated editing and retrieval.

MIX
Papier aus verantwortungsvollen Quellen
Paper from responsible sources
FSC® C105338

If you have any concerns about our products,
you can contact us on
ProductSafety@springernature.com

In case Publisher is established outside the EU,
the EU authorized representative is:
Springer Nature Customer Service Center GmbH
Europaplatz 3, 69115 Heidelberg, Germany

Printed by Libri Plureos GmbH
in Hamburg, Germany